**THE BRIT
HORSE SOC**

GW01339140

DORSET ON H_____

AVAILABLE IN THIS SERIES

The Cotswolds on Horseback
Wiltshire on Horseback
Westmorland on Horseback
The Ridgeway Downs on Horseback
Exmoor on Horseback
Somerset on Horseback
Hampshire on Horseback
Leicestershire & Rutland on Horseback
Humberside on Horseback
Northamptonshire on Horseback
Dorset on Horseback

First published 1995
by The British Horse Society
Access & Rights of Way Department
British Equestrian Centre
Stoneleigh Park, Kenilworth
Warwickshire CV8 2LR

A catalogue record for this book is available from the British Library

ISBN 1 899016 10 4

Printed by:
Tripod Press Limited, 7 Wise Street, Leamington Spa, CV31 3AP

Distribution: The British Horse Society, Stoneleigh Park,
Kenilworth, Warwickshire, CV8 2LR

CONTENTS

	Page No
Acknowledgements	4
Foreword	5
Preface	6
Introduction	8
Introduction to Dorset on Horseback	11
Waymarking and Information	12
The Dorset Network	14
Cranborne Chase	63
Isle of Purbeck	79
The Dorset Downs	95

TRAILS

1.	Corscombe, Halstock, East & West Chelborough - 10 miles	16
2.	Corscombe & Hooke - 12 miles	20
3.	Up Sydling & Sydling St Nicholas - 12 miles	24
4.	Up Cerne - 5.5 miles	28
5.	Piddle Inn Ride - 7.25 miles	32
6.	Piddlehinton & Forston Ride - 10.5 miles	34
7.	Toller Porcorum & West Compton Ride - 9 miles	38
8.	Plush Ride - 7 miles	44
9.	Higher Melcombe & Dorset Gap - 5 miles	48
10.	Eggardon & Powerstock Ride - 12.5 miles	50
11.	Mapperton & Loscombe Ride - 5.75 miles	54
12.	Little Bredy, Bridehead & Sea Ride - 10 miles	56
13.	Hardy's Monument Ride - 7 miles	60
14.	Stubhampton & Ashmore Ride - 12 miles	64
15.	Tarrant Gunville, Harbins Park & Chettle - 11 miles	66
16.	Badbury Ring, Ackling Dyke & Tarrant Monkton - 12 miles	70
17.	Bottle Bush Down, Gussage All Saints, Ackling Dyke - 10 miles	74
18.	Pentridge, Bokerley Ditch & Cranborne - 9 miles	76
19.	Church Knowle Valley Ride - 12 miles	80
20.	The Old Harry Rocks Ride - 17.5 miles	86
21.	Heritage Coastal Ride from East Knighton to Holworth - 13 miles	92
22.	Durweston, Stourpaine, Hod & Hambledon Hills	96
23.	Durweston & Houghton North Down - 8 miles	100
24.	Bulbarrow Hill, Winterborne Houghton & Milton Abbas - 11 miles	102
25.	Bulbarrow Hill, Dorsetshire Gap & Ansty Cross - 9 miles	106

ACKNOWLEDGEMENTS

A number of people and organisations have given their time and expertise to provide details for this book, or contributed in some other material way.

In particular, the British Horse Society would like to thank Jean Heaton and her husband, Vanda Coulsey, Bill Young, Billa Edwards and Debbie Guy for surveying, developing and describing the routes; Zandra Powell for not only surveying and describing rides but also for her excellent illustrations; John Powell for the cover photograph and John Wilkey, Team Leader, Rights of Way Section, Dorset County Council, for his unstinting support, advice and guidance.

Finally, thanks to Philippa Luard and Elwyn Hartley Edwards for their literary contributions.

FOREWORD

When the British Horse Society launched its ARROW Project in 1991, few people could have foreseen the tremendous response and commitment that it would provoke from recreational drivers and riders. That eight trail guide books were in print by May 1994 with the prospect of a further eight in 1995, is testament to their dedication and talent. I am delighted, on behalf of all equestrians, to pay tribute to those who have made such a unique contribution towards the achievement of a network of circular and linear trails.

The Society is concerned that little had been achieved for carriage drivers within ARROW: however it is pleasing that some progress has now been made and that a number of driving trails will be featured this year and in subsequent years.

It is a fact that drivers are restricted to Byways and Unclassified County Roads, thus there are fewer chances to provide them with off-road driving opportunities. This calls for a separate approach, with our Rights of Way staff and volunteers working hand-in-glove with drivers and driving organisations, in order to identify and claim lost routes. The Access & Rights of Way Policy Committee, in overseeing this initiative, will do all in its power to gain maximum benefit for drivers from this important partnership.

As it is virtually impossible to produce a circular or linear route without incorporating some metalled highways it is difficult to lay claim to having opened up a given mileage of 'off-road' riding.

What can be claimed however, is that by the end of 1995 details of up to 350 trails, totalling about 5000 miles, should be in print.

With a further eight books planned for 1996/97 and others in prospect towards the millennium, the Society can, with some justification, feel proud to have contributed to the safety and the greater enjoyment of those who take pleasure from riding and carriage driving.

E A T BONNOR-MAURICE
Chairman, British Horse Society

January 1995

PREFACE

Conditioned as we are to the spread of urban development and its supportive system of trunk roads that encroach, inevitably, upon the countryside, it comes as a surprise to reflect that for well over a thousand years after the withdrawal of the Roman legions no public roads were built in Britain, much less new towns and industrial centres. Indeed, the Roman legacy of 5000 miles (8,000 km) of surfaced via strata did not long survive the departure of its builders. Its lapse into decay was to all intents synonymous with the decline and ultimate eclipse of the beleaguered empire itself.

It was not until 1780 that the system of toll roads had reached that figure again. Fifty years later, thanks principally to the efforts of Telford and McAdam, Britain had 20,000 miles (32,000 km) of good roadways underpinning what became known as the Golden Age of Coaching.

Within the past half-century that road system and the myriad acres of developed areas it services has been multiplied more than a hundred times over, whilst the open countryside and, in consequence, the means of access to it, has been eroded commensurately.

Up to the Industrial Revolution and for many years thereafter, the countryside was crisscrossed with tracks, some of them dating from prehistoric times and other relics of the Roman occupation. They provided trade routes for the transport of every sort of commodity as well as being an essential facility for the traveller. John Wesley, for instance, who led the Methodist revival of the 19th century, reckoned to ride 8000 miles on such tracks in the course of a year. There was, also a comprehensive system of long-distance drove roads, the equivalent of our modern road system, over which thousands and thousands of cattle, sheep, pigs, geese and turkeys were driven to the main centres of population (cattle were shod for the journey and even geese had their webbed feet protected by a pad of tar and sawdust).

The land enclosures of the 18th and 19th centuries took an obvious toll of all kinds of previously public routes and industrial development, dependent on railways, roads and canals, made further inroads into the public rights of access. After that the intensification of farming practice and the sheer speed and scope of urban building were both factors in breaking up the old network of tracks, lanes and paths.

Nonetheless, it was possible, just fifty years ago, for Aime Tschiffely, the archetypal long-distance rider who described his 10,000 mile (16,000 km) two and a half year journey from Buenos Aires to Washington DC in his classic The Tales of Two Horses, to take a 'leisurely jaunt' through England on horseback. The book of that 'jaunt' was called simply Bridle Paths and the idea, he said, was to 'jog along, anyhow and anywhere; canter along quiet country lanes, over hills and through dales - sunshine or rain - alone with a horse to see the real England'

and he could have done the same in Scotland or Wales.

Twenty years after Tschiffely, the broadcaster Wynford Vaughan Thomas made a TV programme of a ride from one end of Wales to the other over the upland ways once traversed by the sad and shadowy princes of that country. Some of those historic routes are no longer open to horsemen, but Wales can still boast the Pilgrim's Ride, the route followed by the devout in their pilgrimage to Bardsey, the island of the Saints, as well as Glyndwr's Way which traverses the most rugged of the upland country. Elsewhere there are other long-distance routes, the South Downs Way, the Pennine and so on, whilst there still remain many shorter routes all over the country that provide the basis for our modern public paths.

Most prominent and active within the environmental lobby seeking to extend and protect the right of off-road riders is the British Horse Society's Access and Rights of Way Committee, co-ordinating the work of over 100 honorary Bridleways Officers in the UK. Amongst its declared objectives, laid down in its National Strategy for Access is 'the establishment of a basic network of public bridleways and byways in all counties, with cross-country and regional links.' It works towards 'linking long distance bridleways in most areas - so that a rider may travel the country if he so desires.'

This handbook with accurate material supplied by local enthusiasts is just one of a series published by the BHS which in the foreseeable future will cover every region of the country, reflecting and reinforcing the need to preserve an invaluable part of our heritage for as long as men and women find their pleasure 'along country lanes, over hills and through dales - sunshine or rain' along with a horse and like-minded companions.

ELWYN HARTLEY EDWARDS
JUNE 1995

INTRODUCTION

The British Horse Society's ARROW Project aims to identify open and usable routes of varying length and shape (circular, figure-of-eight or linear) to help riders and carriage drivers to enjoy the countryside by means, as far as possible, of the network of public rights of way and the minor vehicular highways. This collection of rides is the result of research and mapping by volunteers who took up the challenge of the ARROW initiative with such enthusiasm and effort.

I am faced with the equally daunting challenge of writing an introductory chapter. Should I write reams about each topic or try simply to point you in the right direction? I have decided upon the second method as the search for information is itself highly educative and stays in the mind better than reading it all in one place. Also, since we all have different expectations of our holiday, a very full guide seemed wrong. Nevertheless, there are a few pointers I would like to suggest to you.

The most important one is to start your planning several months in advance of the trip, including a visit to the area you intend to ride in. You should make endless lists of things to DO (e.g. get the saddle checked) and things to CHECK OUT (can you read a map, for instance). You may find joining the local BHS Endurance Riding Group very helpful, as there you will meet people who can give you information about the degree of fitness needed for yourself and your horse (feeding for fitness not dottiness), and many other useful hints on adventurous riding. You may also enjoy some of the Pleasure rides organised by the group or by the local Riding Club. These are usually about 15-20 miles and you ride in company, though using a map. You may find them under the title Training Rides. These rides will get both of you used to going into strange country. If you usually ride on well-known tracks, then your horse will find it nerve-racking to go off into new territory, and you yourself may also find the excitement of deep country a bit surprising, so try to widen your experience at home before you go off on holiday.

ACCOMMODATION

Decide how far you wish to ride each day of your holiday, book overnight accommodation for both of you and if possible visit it to see if the five-star suite on offer to your horse is what he is used to. Decide if you want to stable him or to turn him out at the end of the day, and arrange to drop off some food for him, as he will not relish hard work on a diet of green grass, nor will he enjoy a change in his usual food. If you are to have a back-up vehicle, of course, then you will not need to do some of this, but you should certainly make a preliminary visit if you can. The BHS publish a Bed & Breakfast Guide for Horses which is a list of people willing to accommodate horses, and sometimes riders, overnight. The Society does not inspect these places, so you should check everything in advance.

FITNESS

You and your horse should be fit. For both of you, this is a process taking about two months. If you and/or your horse are not in the full flush of youth, then it may take a bit longer. The office chair, the factory floor, or the household duties do not make or keep you fit, but carefully planned exercise will. Remember that no matter how fit your horse seems, he does not keep himself fit - you get him fit. There are several books with details of fitness programmes for a series of rides. Do not forget to build in a rest day during your holiday - neither of you can keep going all the time, day after day. Miles of walking may get you fit, but it uses different muscles from riding; you may get a surprise when you start riding longer distances. It seems to me that the further you intend to ride, the longer your preparation should be. Nothing can be done in a hurry.

Your horse should be obedient, so work on that. If you want him to stand, then he must stand. If you want to go through water, then he must be prepared to walk down a slope or even step down off a bank to go through the stream, so start with puddles and insist that he go through the middle. Does he help you open gates? I hope so, or you will have a great deal of mounting and dismounting to do. Does he tie up - this is essential if you are to have a peaceful pint at lunchtime.

MAPS

Can you read a map? Can you make and read a grid reference (usually referred to as GR)? Get a Pathfinder map of your area and take yourself for a walk and see if you end up where you expect to. Learn to know exactly where you are on the map, and how to understand the symbols (if your map shows hilly ground, the journey will take longer). Can you work out how long a ride is in miles and roughly how long it will take? You will be using rights of way and it is very important that you stay in the line of the path - that is the only place you have a right to be, and you may deviate from that line only as much as is necessary to get you round an obstruction on the path. You are going to be riding over land that forms

part of someone's work place and that fact must be respected. It is only by the efforts of farmers and landowners that the countryside exists in its present form - so that we may enjoy it as we pass by.

You will need to know the grid reference (GR.) of the start and end of the various tracks you are to use. Get a copy of an Ordnance Survey (OS) Landranger map and really learn the details on the right-hand side, some of which explain how to arrive at a Grid Reference. Learn to go in the door (Eastings - from left to right) and up the stairs (Northings - from bottom to top). There is a great deal of information on the Landranger maps and not so much on the Pathfinders, but the Pathfinder gives more details on the map itself, so that is the map you will use for the actual ride. Or you may care to buy a Landranger of the area you are visiting and, using a highlighter pen, mark in all the rides you want to make, so that you can see through the marks you make. Then get from any Outdoor shop a map case which will allow you to read the map without taking it out of the case and which you can secure round yourself. Also, you should know if you are facing north, south, east or west as you ride. Quite important if you think about it, as it is no good riding into the sunset if you are meant to be going south. Plastic orienteering compasses are cheap and reliable.

TACK

Have your tack thoroughly checked by your saddler, as there is nothing so annoying as a sore back which could have been prevented, or an unnecessarily broken girth strap. How are you going to carry the essential headcollar and rope each day? What about spare shoes, or a false shoe?

What to take on the ride depends on how

much back-up you have. If you have to carry a change of clothes, etc., then you are into very careful planning indeed - balance saddle bag, the lot. If you are based at your first night stop all the time, then life is much easier. You should always carry a first aid kit for horse and rider. You will also have to plan how to wash the girth and numnah. Remember our delightful climate and always carry a waterproof and additional warm clothing - it never pays to gamble with rain and wind.

SAFETY

It is always wiser to ride in company. The other person can always hold your horse, or pull you out of the ditch, as well as being someone to talk to about the excitements of the day and to help plan everything. You should always wear a BSI riding hat, properly secured, and also safe footwear. You need a clearly defined heel and a smooth sole. Even if riding in company, tell someone where you are going and roughly how long you expect to take. If affordable, take a portable telephone. Make a list of the things you must carry every day and check it before leaving base.

INSURANCE

You should have Third Party Legal Liability Insurance. This will protect you if you or your horse cause a bit of mayhem (accidentally!). Membership of the BHS gives you this type of insurance, plus Personal Accident Insurance as part of the membership package. Check your household insurance to make sure it covers riding before you rely only on that, as some-insurances do not. You should always have this type of cover when venturing forth into the outside world, even if it is an hours hack from home.

PARKING

If you intend to box to the start of the day's ride, either have someone to take the box away or make sure it is safely, securely and considerately parked. If you have to make arrangements to park, do it well in advance or the contact may well have gone to market or the hairdressers when you make a last minute call. Have the vehicle number etched on to the windows for security.

MONEY

This is vital, so work out a system of getting money if necessary. Sadly we can no longer gallop up to the bank and lead Dobbin into the cashier's queue, nor do most banks have hitching rails. Post Offices are more numerous and might be a useful alternative. Always have the price of a telephone call on you.

Lastly, if you do run into problems of blocked paths or boggy ones, write to the Highway Authority of the relevant county council and tell them. Then you can do something about it. You might even think of adopting a path near home and keeping an eye on it, telling your own county council of any difficulties you encounter. It is through such voluntary work that these rides have been made possible.

Wherever you ride, always do it responsibly, with care of the land, consideration for the farmer and courtesy for all other users. Remember the Country Code and enjoy your ARROW Riding.

I hope this chapter will have started you planning and making lists. If I seem to be always writing about forward planning it is only because I usually leave things to the last minute, which causes chaos!

PHILIPPA LUARD

INTRODUCTION TO
DORSET ON HORSEBACK

Dorset is one of the loveliest counties in Britain. To explore the many bridleways on horseback, is to experience a ride back in time. If you were to ride around the whole county, each day would bring a subtle change of scenery: each range of hills another lovely view. The valleys too are full of secret delights.

The heart of Dorset consists of rolling chalk hills with a steep escarpment in the north overlooking the Blackmore Vale (where bridleways are scarce.) Villages were built mostly in the valleys: the Saxon town of Shaftesbury at 700 feet is one of the exceptions.

Roads follow valley bottoms or along the top of high ground and small lanes are flanked by hedges grown on flower covered banks.

Dorset shows much evidence of early man: on the high chalk ridges are many hill forts: Maiden Castle, Badbury Rings, Bulbarrow, Eggardon and Pilsden Pen - the highest point in the county (scene of commercial rabbit farming from the medieval period to the 17th century!). Hardy's Monument dominates the southern skyline. Commemorating the Vice Admiral of Nelsons' "Kiss me Hardy" fame, the site

is one of the points from which the first triangulation of the country was measured and chosen by Hardy for a sea mark of furze faggots.

The coastline is dramatic: from the high cliffs of Golden Cap, to the spectacular Fleet - the lagoon behind Chesil Bank - from the bleak heights of Portland to Poole Harbour - one of the largest natural harbours in the world. All this you can enjoy from the back of a horse - but choose a fine day!

In East Dorset bridleways follow the Frome water meadows, cross heathland - sadly much depleted since the novels of Thomas Hardy - lead through Wareham Forest and follow lanes and downland tracks up to the medieval forest of Cranborne Chase in the north east. Crossing chalk downland above the Blackmore Vale, bridleways lead south to the rich agricultural land of West Dorset, with its lovely valleys and hills.

Wherever you ride, spectacular views unfold. Tiny hamlets lie amid remnants of medieval settlements; old sunken lanes wait to be explored and stretches of downland turf invite long canters.

WAYMARKING & INFORMATION

Dorset has many bridleways and the job of opening and clearing and waymarking is far from completed at the time of writing. The rides in this book are mostly waymarked off the roads - usually with a blue arrow in a white disk and sometimes an old blob of blue paint - but many still wait to be signed across farmland. It is essential to read the instructions carefully and to follow the map. All these routes are open and ridden.

There are still smallholdings in West Dorset and one stretch of bridleway may cross land belonging to several owners. Riders are requested to be particularly considerate to the needs of smallholders - and larger stock and arable farmers. Many gates are far from ideal and much tactful work has still to be done to ensure good relations when long closed Rights of Way are opened up through the predominantly sheep and dairy farms. But all these beautiful rides are more than worth the effort of dismounting for a gate, walking through stock, or time spent in friendly acknowledgement of the owner of the land.

Some of these routes are remote and do not include a pub or shop en route - be prepared to take a picnic.

Do not forget to look back at the view behind you - as well as the panorama unrolling ahead. All Dorset is waiting for you to explore - on horseback!

Looking north to the Piddle Valley

CODE FOR RIDING & DRIVING RESPONSIBLY

THE BRITISH
HORSE SOCIETY

1. **Riders and carriage drivers** everywhere should proceed with courtesy, care and consideration. The British Horse Society recommends the following:

    Care for the Land
    > Do not stray off the line of the path;
    > Do not damage timber or hedgerows by jumping;
    > Remember that horses' hooves can damage surfaces in bad weather;
    > Pay particular attention to protected areas that have significant historical and/or biological value, as they are extremely sensitive to damage.

    Courtesy to other users
    > Remember that walkers, cyclists and other riders may be elderly, disabled, children or simply frightened of horses; whenever possible acknowledge courtesy shown by drivers of motor vehicles.

    Consideration for the farmer
    > Shut the gate behind you;
    > Ride slowly past all stock;
    > Do not ride on cultivated land unless the right of way crosses it;
    > Dogs are seldom welcome on farmland or moorland unless on a lead or under close control.

2. **Observe local byelaws**

3. **Ride or drive with care on the roads** and take the BHS Riding and Road Safety Test. Always make sure that you can be seen at night or in bad visibility, by wearing the right kind of reflective/ fluorescent aids.

4. **Groups from riding establishments** should contain reasonable numbers, for reasons of both safety and amenity. They should never exceed twenty in total **including** the relevant number of escorts as indicated in BHS guidelines on levels of capability among riders in groups, available on request. Rides should not deviate from the right of way or permitted route and regard must be shown at all times for growing crops, shutting and securing of gates and the consideration and courtesy due to others.

5. **Always obey the Country Code in every way possible:**
    > Enjoy the countryside and respect its life and work
    > Guard against all risk of fire
    > Fasten all gates
    > Keep your dogs under close control
    > Keep to public paths across farmland
    > Use gates and stiles to cross fences, hedges and walls
    > Leave livestock, crops and machinery alone
    > Take your litter home
    > Help keep all water clean
    > Protect wildlife, plants and trees
    > Take special care on country roads
    > Make no unnecessary noise.

DORSET
ON HORSEBACK

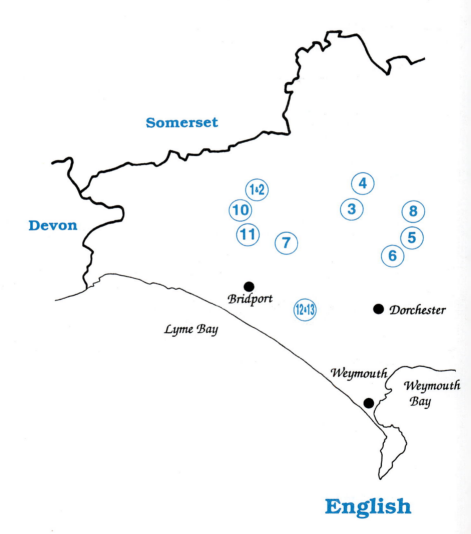

Somerset

Devon

1·2

10

11

7

4

3

8

5

6

Bridport

12·13

Dorchester

Lyme Bay

Weymouth

Weymouth
Bay

English

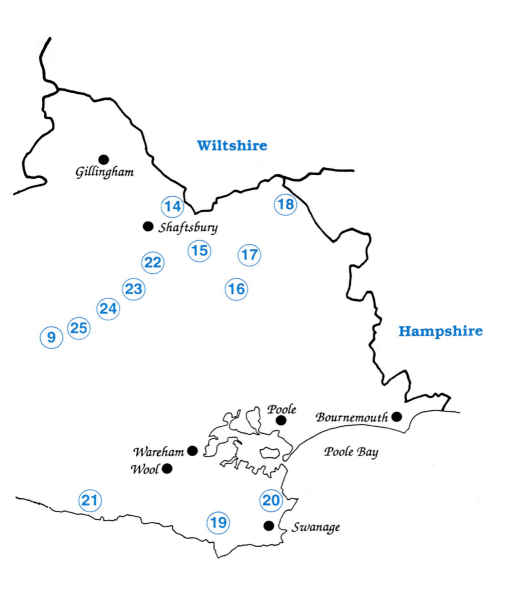

Wiltshire

● Gillingham

⑭

● Shaftsbury

⑮ ⑰

⑱

㉒

⑯

㉓

㉔

⑨ ㉕

Hampshire

Poole
●
Bournemouth ●

Wareham ●

Poole Bay

Wool ●

㉑

⑳

⑲

● Swanage

Channel

CORSCOMBE, HALSTOCK, EAST & WEST CHELBOROUGH

TRAIL 1

A 10 MILE CIRCULAR TRAIL (CLOCKWISE)

Ordnance Survey Maps:
Landranger: 194
Pathfinder: 1298

Parking & Starting Point:
Parking is available by prior arrangement with Mrs Powell at Catsley Farm, Corscombe. (GR.526039). Please telephone: 01935 891220.

Of Interest:
This is a most delightful ride with breathtaking views in all directions. You can't even see a busy road! The route is totally devoid of bridleway signposts, but most gates have a waymark. This is a beautiful ride with high vantage points and lovely coombes and rolling hills. There are many rights of way all around this area and in Dorset generally, and by studying the map, it would be easy to lengthen, change, shorten or vary the route to your own individual taste and time available.

Route Description:

Turn left out of Catsley Farm. After a few yards, turn right down a grass track. At the bottom of the track, turn left past the cottage (GR.523045), go through the metal gate and into the field. Keep the wood on your left until you reach a hunting gate. Go through the gate and ride straight ahead on the same line, going diagonally up the coombe and through a field gate. Continue

diagonally across the next field to a hunting gate (GR.512045). Cross the road here and go through the field gate immediately opposite. Take the bridleway diagonally to your right, going north across the field to a hunting gate in a wire fence. Go through the gate and ride carefully down a short, very steep, hill to the

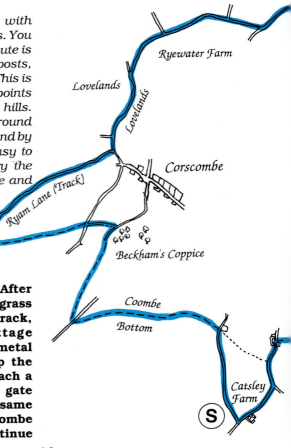

Ryewater Farm

Lovelands

Lovelands

Corscombe

Ryam Lane (Track)

Beckham's Coppice

Coombe Bottom

Catsley Farm

(S)

bottom. Keep right and go through the hunting gate facing you. Pass some old standing stones on your left, through the gate and straight on, on the lower grassy track below wooden chalets. This leads up to another track (GR.515052).

Turn left and follow this stony track for some 400 yards to a road. Turn left and very shortly go through a field gate on the right and into the field. Ride straight ahead passing between a spinney on the right and trees in a field on your left, following the usually defined grassy track going westward.

Keep the spinney on the right until you come to a waymarked gateway into a field where a steep ridged hill faces you. Ride on keeping the hedge on your left, climbing and turn steeply right in front of the hedge to keep the hedge on your left until you reach a field gate that brings you out into Ryam Lane, which is a grassy track (GR.505049).

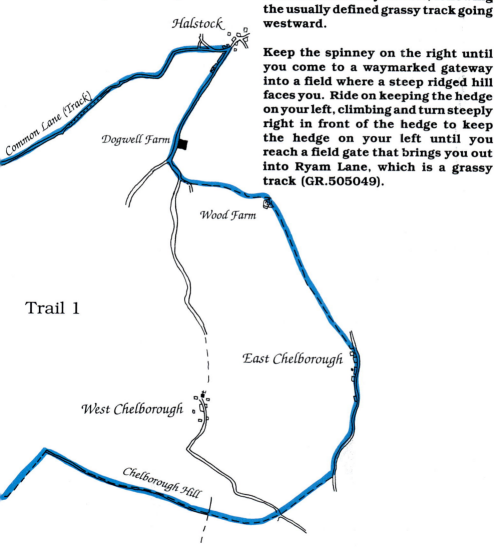

Halstock

Common Lane (Track)

Dogwell Farm

Wood Farm

Trail 1

East Chelborough

West Chelborough

Chelborough Hill

Turn right and follow down this track for approximately one mile to the road into Corscombe (GR.513057).

Turn left and follow the small road for 0.75 miles, ignoring the 'No Through Road' on the left to Weston, until you come to a sharp left bend. Go straight on and into the track (GR.516066). After approximately 0.50 miles, stay left at the junction of tracks (GR.523068). *This common lane is wide and shady and goes for approximately two miles to Halstock. You will pass a golf course to your left.* **When you reach Halstock turn right on the village road.** The Post Office and Shop is on your left and some 100 yards further on, a T-junction with The Quiet Woman Public House. Turn right and follow the road for about 0.50 miles.

After crossing the small bridge (GR.538079) take the first turn left signed Crockermoor and keep left on the metalled track where a grassy bridleway goes off to your right. Go through the first double metal gates on your left. *These are tricky to shut so please take care to make sure they are closed.* Head for a telegraph pole in the centre of the field and go through the gate beyond. Ride straight across the next field to a hunting gate, stream and another hunting gate and then go right up a bank and across a field to go through a gate to the left of a farmyard.

Turn right through the farm yard, passing between the house and farm buildings. (GR.544069). This is Wood Farm. Out of the farm yard go left and through another gate. Ride over the first field to go through the left-hand gate and then continue diagonally left to the top corner where a hunting gate will be found which leads to approximately 20 yards of track and into a field. *This small section can sometimes be overgrown.*

Keeping the hedge on the left, continue to the next hunting gate. Ride straight on with the barbed wire fence on the left. You may encounter electric fence before Manor Farm at East Chelborough (GR.553059), which is not connected and can be taken down. *Along this high point you have a good view of Castle Hill ahead and to your right you can see the entire circuit you have ridden.* Go through the left-hand gate and into the cattle yard, leaving through a gate onto a road. Turn right and ride for about 0.50 miles, keeping a watch for a small chalky pit - sometimes there is silage in it. Having passed this, take the second gate on the right which is waymarked on the right-hand post (GR.553050), into a track and field.

Leaving the track, cross diagonally over the field heading for a wood, to a metal gate leading onto a metalled lane (GR.548047). Turn right, then immediately left, and immediately right up a peaty track and go through the hunting gate at the top. Keep the coppice on your right to the next field gate. *Beware when opening the gate, the wire field fence is electrified!* Continue slightly left-handed across the next field to a hunting gate.

Go through this, keep the hedge and the barn on your left and go through another field gate. With the hedge and wire on your left here, go through another field gate. The Chelborough Woods are now down to your right. Continue on the same line, keeping the fence on your left until you reach another field gate that brings you into a green track which is hedged on either side. Follow this, bending hard left at the elbow (GR.532049) and ride along this lane until you reach New House Farm (GR.527045). Turn left along the road and continue to the signpost. Take the right fork and Catsley Farm and your starting point is the second property on the left.

THE HALSTOCK SHOP

A 12 MILE CIRCULAR TRAIL (CLOCKWISE)

Ordnance Survey Maps:
Landranger: 194
Pathfinder: 1298

Parking & Starting Point:
Parking is available by prior arrangement with Mrs A Thompson, Higher Langdon Farm, Beaminster, Dorset. Please telephone 01308 862573 (GR.506025).

Alternative parking is available by prior arrangement with Mr & Mrs H Powell, Catsley Farm, Corscombe, Dorset (GR.526039). Please telephone 01935 891220. If parking here, join the ride by turning right out of Catsley Farm, then left at the signpost and right in the farmyard. This track joins the route (GR.532048) above the drained bridleway. You are now able to complete a circular route from Catsley Farm by continuing straight on when the track bends sharply right back down to Higher Langdon Farm.

Route Description:

From Higher Langdon Farm, ride up the metal track and where it bends left at the top, turn right onto a grassy track which leads into a field. Go into the field and keep the hedge on your right until you come to another gate. Go through this gate and into a lane which brings you out onto a road (GR.496030). Cross straight over the road and go through the gate into a field. Now keep the hedge on your left and continue until you come to the end of the field where you will meet another road (GR.492034). Cross over the road and turn right-handed through a hunting gate which has a waymark and into a field. Keeping the hedge on your left, ride for the whole length of the field, going right-handed at the end still keeping the hedge on your left. You will come out onto a metalled track. Turn left and then right, along a grassy track (GR.495038). *This land belongs to the Donkey Sanctuary, but the fields are used to make hay and silage, and so for much of the time, not grazing donkeys!*

Follow this grassy track through two gateways and continue with the track now hedged on both sides, until you reach a hunting gate leading into a large field. Keep the hedge on your right here for two sides of the field until you reach the A356 (GR.505047). Emerge with care onto the road and turn left then, almost immediately, turn right into Ryam Lane which is a grassy lane. Ride as far as the first metal field gate on the right. Go through this gate and keep the hedge on your right along the top of the field. *There are spectacular views of Corscombe, or Bogs Bottom as it is sometimes called, on your left.*

Drop steeply down, still with the hedge on your right, bending left at

the end of the field, and head for the field gateway ahead. Go into the next field and follow the faint grassy track with the coppice on your left, until you reach a short stretch of stony track going downhill where you can see the field gate beyond which leads onto a road (GR.513052). Turn left and very soon turn right along a stony track, leaving the chalets to your right. Stay on the track where you can see a trout farm below you on the right. This track leads down to the road in Corscombe (GR.518055). Turn right and continue for about 0.50 miles through the village. Turn left into the unsigned road in front of the new housing estate (GR.522053). Continue to the T-junction and turn left onto the road and ride on until you come to the Fox Inn (GR.526054).

Keep straight on, leaving the Fox Inn on the right and Corscombe Court on the left to take the right turn with a 'No Through Road' sign and letter box. Pass houses on the right and continue as far as Norwood Cottage, which you will see in front of you. The metalled road bends left, but you turn right before the cottage and go through a gate into a field (GR.531054). Follow the grassy track with the wood to your left, and when you reach the wire fence, turn right up the bank, keeping the hedge on the left. At the top, go through the hunting gate and onto a track. *Stay in single file here as the track was a bad bog but has now been drained down the middle.*

At the top you come to a stonier bridleway (GR.532048). Turn left along this bridleway, which becomes grassy, and continue until it meets a field. Go through the gate and onward on the same line, keeping the hedge and fence on the right. Ride into the next field, still with the fence on your right, following the track uphill, into the next field. Continue straight on, with the barn and hedge on the right. At the end of this field you will come to a hunting gate. Go through this gate and continue riding straight ahead across the field towards the wood, which you keep on your left.

When you come to the field gate, go carefully through - there is electrified wire in the fence line at the side of the gate as you open it. Continue through the next field with the wood on the left and ride down until you come to a hunting gate leading into a steep, peaty pathway going down hill and onto a farm track. Turn left and immediately right and follow this road to the cross roads known as Grexy Cross (GR.554045) where you turn right and continue along the road to the Red Post. *This is allegedly haunted by Cromwell's mounted horsemen!* Turn right and continue to Benville Bridge - *read the notice on the bridge!*

Turn left after Benville Bridge and after about 100 yards, look for the bridleway on the right. This is Yard Drove, but the entrance can be difficult to see as it is between two hedges (GR.553037). *This old Drove is actually quite wide but the growth can make it narrow and twisty in parts. It is quite lovely, particularly with the bluebells in the spring and it is over a mile long. The Drove bends round to the left and emerges on Linnet Lane (GR.544025).* Turn right along this small road and continue for approximately 0.25 miles with the grass verge on the left, riding as far as the A356 road (GR.536024).

Cross straight over onto a track and continue riding past the barn and down to the cross-country course on your right . Where the track turns sharply right uphill, you carry straight on along the line of the cross-country fences with the hedge on your left. *Along this stretch there is sometimes electric fencing - go through it using the insulated handles.* Go through the next gateway and continue with the hedge to the left, through the next gateway, taking care to avoid the overgrown cattle grid which lies to the right-hand side of the gate. Continue across the paddock riding beside the hedge to the left and onto a concrete track. Turn left and ride downhill to Hooke, where you come out onto the road by a trout farm (GR.534005).

Turn right and ride for about 0.75 miles along the road. Continue past the pond on the right and Hooke Court on the left until you come to a T-junction (GR.527000). Turn right and follow the road keeping Hooke Wood on the left. *This is the furniture maker, John Makepeace's 'working woodland!'*

At the small junction keep left at the "No Through Road" sign and continue to ride for approximately 0.50 miles to turn right on to the waymarked bridleway which goes through rough ground by a small lay-by (GR.513007). Ride along here until you come to the B3163 road at Dirty Gate. Cross straight over this to the metalled track which has a good grass verge on the right. *The most wonderful views to the left: Beaminster*

lies below you and you can see Golden Cap and the sea.

Follow this track until it bends hard right back to Higher Langdon Farm and your starting point.

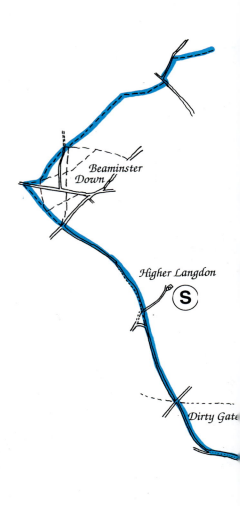

22

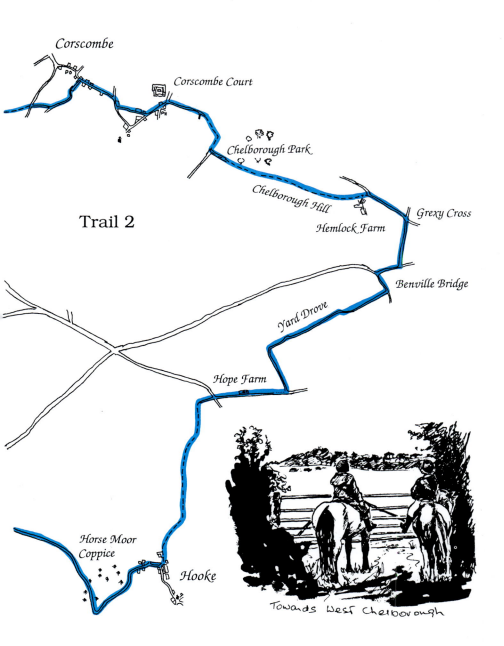

Corscombe

Corscombe Court

Chelborough Park

Trail 2

Chelborough Hill

Hemlock Farm

Grexy Cross

Benville Bridge

Yard Drove

Hope Farm

Horse Moor
Coppice

Hooke

Towards West Chelborough

23

**A 12 MILE CIRCULAR TRAIL
(ANTI-CLOCKWISE)**

Ordnance Survey Maps:
Pathfinders: 1299 & 1318
Landranger: 194

*NOTE: It is not advised to attempt
this ride during the shooting season
in the winter months.*

Parking & Starting Point:
Parking is available at the Batcombe
Down picnic area on Gore Hill
(GR.635038).

Route Description:

**Leave the parking area at the south
end and turn right on to the road,
then almost immediately turn left
onto a track which is directly
opposite the lane down hill to your
right, signed 'The Friary'. Continue
along this path which is hedged and
fenced on both sides, until you come
to a flinty farm track coming in from
the right (GR.638033). Turn left
along this track.** *There is a spectacular
view here if you look down into the 'bowl'
below.* **Keep to the right on the farm
track by a field entrance ahead.
Keep sharp right again where the
grassy track continues straight on.
Follow this stony track all the way
down to Up Sydling, passing a Dutch
barn on the left. Ignore other
bridleway signs to the left.** *You will
see the village of Sydling St Nicholas in
the valley ahead, this is your destination.
It is not advisable to do more than*
a walk along this stony track, *but
this does allow time to enjoy the lovely
views.*

**Continue downhill ignoring paths
going off to the left. The hamlet of
Up Sydling is at the bottom of the
hill (GR.632013). Stay to the left of
the triangle, keeping the post and
rail fence on the right. At the small
road junction, keep straight ahead
riding through the ford.** *This is never
deep and sometimes even dry.* **Ride
along this road for about 1.75 miles
to the cross roads and go straight
across, to enter the long and pretty
village of Sydling St Nicholas. Ride
through the middle of the village,
ignoring the road to the left signed
to Cerne Abbas.**

*In the middle of the village you will find
the Greyhound Inn and a telephone box
opposite. The stream runs beside the
road and the village has an abundance
of lovely cottages, many with bridges to
the road.*

**Continue to ride along the main
street;** *this is the Dorchester road;*
**passing East Street on the left and a
road to the right leading to the
church. On leaving the village, there
is a pair of cottages on the left where
the stream goes under the road and
a bridleway sign is on the left
(GR.633989). Turn left here and
almost immediately turn right to the
farm, signed 'Huish'. Go through the
white gateway, keeping the
attractive brick wall of Huish**

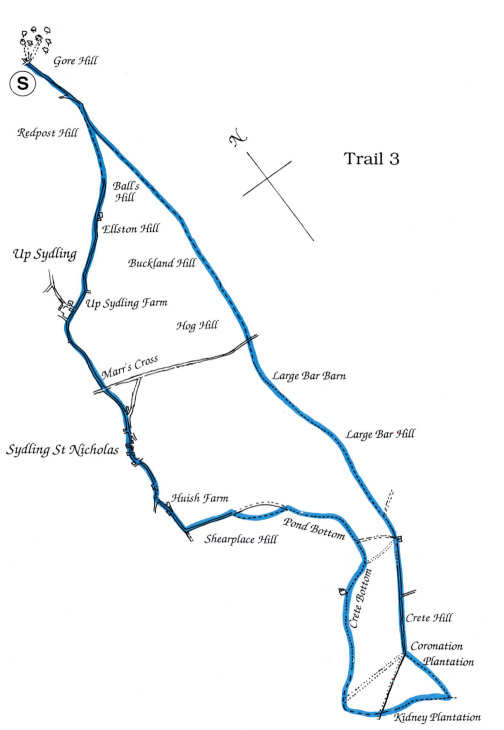

Gore Hill

S

Redpost Hill

Ball's Hill

Ellston Hill

Up Sydling

Buckland Hill

Up Sydling Farm

Hog Hill

Marr's Cross

Large Bar Barn

Large Bar Hill

Sydling St Nicholas

Huish Farm

Shearplace Hill

Pond Bottom

Crete Bottom

Crete Hill

Coronation Plantation

Kidney Plantation

N

Trail 3

25

Farmhouse on the left. The track goes through the farmyard, passing a brick cottage on the right before going left uphill on another stony track, at the sheep run and farm buildings on the left.

Follow the track as it climbs uphill. Keep straight on at the junction of tracks at the top, going downhill on a fenced track. Continue downhill through a gateway with sheep fencing on the right and ride along Crete Bottom. Follow the bottom of the valley through waymarked gateways - not always in the most obvious place! There are other bridleways going off this track, but you stay ahead on the obvious route with sheep fencing on the right, and continue along the valley bottom. On reaching a large barn on the right, turn right through the field gate in front of the barns and take the first gate on the left to leave the barns behind on the right. Continue along the valley bottom with sheep wire again on the right and ignore the faint grassy track going off diagonally up to the left.

Ride on to the next field gate, through this and on along the same line still with sheep fencing to the right. Go through another field gate and continue as before. Ride over one more field and, where the track bends hard left, up hill, turn right through a waymarked gate and onto another obvious grassy track, again with sheep fencing on the right.

Do not take the track into the wood, but stay straight ahead keeping the wood on the right - the track is now not so well defined. Continue until a hedge faces you (GR.644963). Turn left up the hill keeping the hedge on the right - until you come to a hunting gate on the right about 100 yards up.

Go through this gate and continue straight ahead with a new plantation and big hedge on the right. Ignore the hunting gate with a bridleway waymark which is on the right and continue straight on until you are about two-thirds of the way across the field, when you will reach an obvious undisturbed bridleway going off up hill to the left. Turn left here and continue to ride to the top of the hill. Here there is a cross roads of bridleways (GR.649960). Ride straight ahead and into the wooded area for 100 yards.

Take the slightly left hand track leaving the barn on the right. Continue along a grassy track to a field gate and turn left through the gate and go through another field gate and continue along an obvious track with a big hedge on the left. When you meet the farm track with the barn to your left (GR.653964), keep left. Continue along this track which is fenced on both sides, go through the field gate and turn right through another gate into a green lane which is hedged on both sides.

When the track bends hard to the right, continue to ride straight ahead through the gateway and into another green lane which is waymarked. Go out of the lane and through the next field keeping the hedge on the right. Ignore the gate on the right and continue on to a waymarked hunting gate which is in the corner of the field.

Continue to ride ahead, bearing slightly left. Where the hedge juts out into the field you will see a hunting gate. Go through this gate and keep the hedge on the left. About half way along this hedge on the left you will find a hunting gate. Go through this gate and continue with the hedge on the right. Go through the next field gate and across the top of the next field keeping to the track by the side of the right hand hedge. Continue along this track until you come to a road where there is a bungalow with farm buildings (GR.647003).

Cross straight over the road and onto a grassy track with a fence to the left and a hedge on the right. Ride along this track past a radio mast on the right and with the valley below on the left. Ignore any tracks going off to the left. When you meet the stony track you came along on your outward journey, ride straight ahead. At the head of the coombe, with the valley below to the left, take the signed bridleway which lies half right, through the bushes, away from the main track. You are now retracing your steps along this lane to the road. At the road turn right and in a short distance turn left into Batcombe picnic area where the ride started.

Up Sydling ford

UP CERNE

TRAIL 4

A 5.50 MILE CIRCULAR TRAIL (CLOCKWISE)

Ordnance Survey Map:
Pathfinder: 1299
Landranger: 194

Parking & Starting Point:
Parking is available at the Batcombe picnic site on Gore Hill (GR.635038).

Route Description:

Ride through the picnic area to the road and turn left. Continue along the road until the trees on the left come to an end. *The bridleway starts here and not as shown on the Ordnance Survey maps. The route was diverted away from the wood because of the massive flints which were turned up when the original bridleway was ploughed. The bridleway now runs next to the road and is a grassy track.*

Ride along here for about 0.25 miles. When the field ends and the road continues straight on (GR.646048), follow the track right, still going round the field, with the hedge on the left. Continue along this grassy track at the top edge of the field until you reach a wooded area. Ride straight on here through trees. *On top of the ridge there is a beautiful view to the right and Mintern House is just visible through the trees to the left.*

On reaching a definite fork in the track (GR.656036), just after a hunting gate on the left and by a large oak tree, go right, down the hill. Follow this track down to the bottom of the hill, ignoring the track joining it from the right. The track turns grassy and runs along an avenue of trees with open fields on either side. At the bottom, turn left on a hard metal track (GR.654031) and ride towards Up Cerne Manor and hamlet. *On the left is a pretty Georgian house.*

On reaching a T-junction of tracks with the driveway to the manor ahead (GR.658028), turn right. Continue to ride down the road through an avenue of trees and open fields on either side. On reaching the T-junction (GR.655025), the road goes left. Here your route goes right on a chalky track which is followed uphill.

Pass a clump of trees on the left and continue on until the scrappy hedge ends and a broken gate post is on the left (GR.648025). Turn left here on to the track and follow it round to the right, keeping the hedge on the right and the woodland on the left. At the end of the wooded area, ignore a faint track going down to the left and keep straight on the track.

Where there is a field ahead, ride straight across the middle on the same line. At the far end of the field, go through a gap in the hedge and turn right on a green track in between a hedge and wire fence

28

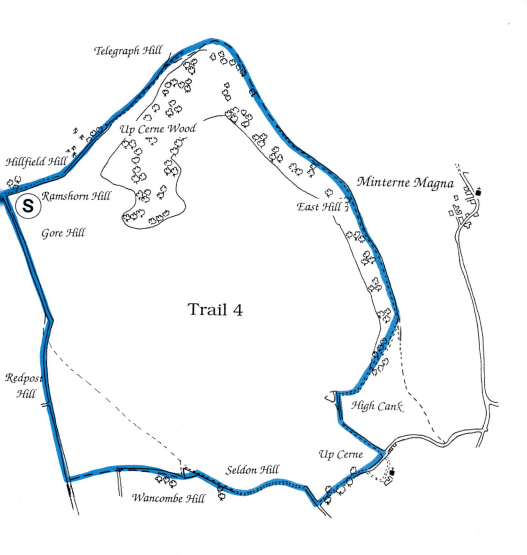

Trail 4

(GR.642024). **This is a cross roads of bridleways. Continue on this track riding straight on ignoring other tracks that come in from the left.** *This section of the route is marked with a Wessex Ridgeway sign.*

Where the coombe on the left comes to a head, as the track bends slightly left, take a small track half right going through the bushes in an open bushy area, following the waymarker. DO NOT CONTINUE ON THE MAIN TRACK PAST THE BARNS. Continue on this track until you come to the road where you turn right and your parking place is on the left.

UP CERNE MA

A 7.25 MILE CIRCULAR TRAIL (CLOCKWISE)

Ordnance Survey Maps:
Pathfinder: 1318
Landranger: 194

Parking & Starting Points:
Parking is available in a small lay-by on the left of Rectory Road, Piddlehinton (GR.713971). Rectory Road leads west out of the village. Alternative parking can be found if you turn right off Rectory Road into Paynes Close in the small County Council Car Park on the right, or leave the village on Rectory Road and park on the grass verge which is further out of the village.

NB: At a steady walk and trot, this ride takes about 90 minutes.

Route Description:

From your parking place ride down Rectory Road into the village and turn left onto a track (GR.714972) which lies between two cottages just beyond West Lane Cottage and opposite the Old Rectory door in the high wall. Continue along this track for about 0.50 miles going through a gate until you come to a T-junction. Go through another gate and turn right and ride down this track until you come to another gate on your left and go through to ride along the edge of the field past a white mill house on the right, riding for about 0.25 miles to another gate leading down on to a road. Cross over the road and continue riding straight on down a track, leaving a big barn on the right.

Follow the track, turning right at the T-junction, along the valley. After about 400 yards, go straight on into a grassy lane, where the main track goes to the right, ending at a 5-bar gate at a cottage.

When you reach here you have actually ridden along behind the villages of Piddlehinton and White Lackington, to Piddletrenthide whose name comes from the River Piddle and its assessment for thirty hides at Domesday. The stone and flint cottages in this area are of 17th and 18th century origin - later buildings are banded in flint and brick. The Church of All Saints has a tower dated 1487 and a 15th century porch with a Norman doorway.

Go through the 5-bar gate by the cottage and continue straight across a field to another gate leading on to a farm road. Fifty yards beyond two farm cottages, turn right through a 5-bar gate. Continue along by a hedgerow on the right and go through three wicket gates above the playing fields on the right riding until you reach a grassy field. Ride diagonally to your left through a gateway and then diagonally to your right down to a 5-bar gate into a lane. Bear right along the grassy track to the river. Walk along IN the river to your right until you reach The Piddle Inn, where refreshments are available (GR.704997).

From The Piddle Inn, turn right on to the road. Ride for 200 yards and then turn left up the track marked Tullons Lane, with a cottage called 'Long Acre' on the left. Ride up the steep hill for about one mile, continuing straight on when the track narrows down to a grassy lane between hedges, ignoring the main track going to the right. At the T-junction at the end of this grassy lane (GR.722001) turn right riding past a clump of trees on your left and continue for approximately 0.50 miles to a wicket gate. Keep straight on along the obvious track and fork left before the bushes to keep the bushy hedge on the left. Continue to ride downhill, following the track round to the right along the valley bottom. Stay right at the fork with the line of the copse to the left, and continue for about one mile until another track is reached.

With a wicket gate on the left, turn right along a narrow track between sloe bushes until arriving at another wicket gate into a wood, known as Doles Wood. Follow the track through the bottom of the wood staying right in the wood when another bridleway comes in from a field ahead. Leave the wood, crossing a track to go up the hill and down to a tarmaced road, round double iron gates. Continue to ride up the hill past a piggery and grain drier on the left, and carry on until you come to the main valley road.

Cross straight over the road and the River Piddle into Rectory Road and so return to your parking place.

A 10.50 MILES CIRCULAR TRAIL (CLOCKWISE)

Ordnance Survey Map:

Pathfinder: 1318
Landranger: 194

Parking & Starting Point:

Parking is available in a small lay-by on the left of Rectory Road, Piddlehinton (GR.713971). Rectory Road leads west out of the village. Alternative parking can be found if you turn right off Rectory Road into Paynes Close in the small County Council Car Park on the right, or leave the village on Rectory Road and park on the grass verge which is further out of the village.

Route Description:

Ride down Rectory Road and into the village to turn left (GR.714972) into a track that lies between two cottages just beyond West Lane Cottage and opposite the Old Rectory door in the high wall. Continue along this track for about 0.50 miles to a T-junction (GR.712978). Turn left going uphill on another green lane. In 50 yards go through a gateway to continue riding up the hill for approximately 0.25 miles to another gate. Go through this gate and into the field. Continue straight on with the hedge on your right, on the headland, to a heavy metal gate. Here there is a crossroads of bridleways.

Go through the gate and stay on the

main track which bends sharp left down hill (GR.702975) and then go uphill to bend hard right at the top. Continue for about 300 yards after the bend and turn left uphill towards some farm buildings to come to a road (GR.699967).

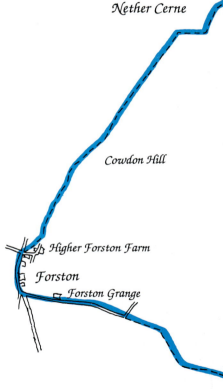

Nether Cerne

Cowdon Hill

Higher Forston Farm

Forston

Forston Grange

Cross straight over this road and onto a concrete track going downhill and then continue uphill on a stony track, leaving the farm building on

the left. Continue on this track going through a gateway with a hedge on the left and arable fields on the right. On the brow of the hill, leave the main track going left and continue riding straight ahead on the headland of the field with the wire fence on the left. Follow the track through the field to a metal gate in the second side of the field, on the left, and into another cultivated field.

Turn left and, keeping the hedge on the left, continue to a little copse on the left, where there is a narrow metal gate with a bridleway sign (GR.699954). Go through this gate into the copse to emerge into a field. Stay left and ride downhill on the headland with the wire fence on the left. A large spinney, Wolfeton Clump, is on the right.

Trail 6

At the bottom of the hill, ignore the marked bridleway on the left and continue straight ahead on the headland, now rising slightly with a hedge on the left. At the top of the hill go through a gateway and turn immediately right (GR.698947). Ride along this headland with the hedge on the right. At the kink in the hedge, continue straight ahead along the obvious grass track. Go through the gap so that the hedge is now on the left.

When this hedge ends, continue straight ahead on the grassy track which now goes uphill over an open

35

field. Go through the metal gate ahead and on along the headland keeping the hedge on your left. Keep on ahead and go through another metal gate and continue some 100 yards along the track, with the hedge now on your right, to another gate. Go through this gate, which is rather heavy, and onto the road (GR.685952). *The traffic here is light, but can be fast.* Cross straight over the road with care. Go along the track ahead for 200 yards to another small road. Cross over this and into a bridleway, signposted 'Forston Grange 1 mile'. *On the left is the large building which housed the old Herrison Hospital.*

Continue down hill along this green lane, bending round to the left, to the bottom where there is a gate. Go through this gate bearing left and then follow the headland with the hedge on the left, uphill again, to a barn at the top on the right. Join the stony track straight ahead which is hedged on both sides and ride downhill to Forston Grange Farm at the bottom.

Go through the farmyard and bend left to cross on the little bridge over the River Cerne to the main valley road in Forston (GR.665956). Turn right and ride up this road for about 300 yards. Turn right over a brick parapeted bridge, re-crossing the River Cerne. There is a red letter box in the wall on the right and large wrought iron gates ahead. Go through the waymarked wooden 5-bar gate to the left of the iron gates, into Higher Forston Farm.

The bridleway goes straight through this property, so please ride with great consideration and take care

to stay on the driveway. Please do not ride on the garden. Leave through the wooden gate from the driveway and follow the track straight ahead, with the river down to your left. Do not go through the gate facing you, but continue to the right of this, keeping the high hedge on your left and the hill up on the right. On reaching the waymarked gate at the end of the field ahead of you, go through and ride diagonally to the right up Cowdon Hill, with the ragged hedge and fence on the right. At the top of the hill is a gate in the right hand corner.

Below on the left is the village of Godmanstone and the Smiths Arms public house. This is featured in the Guinness Book of Records as being the smallest public house in England. It is 39 feet long, 12 feet high and 14 feet wide. Granted a licence in 1661 by King Charles II the building is 15th century. Unfortunately at this point, only a footpath descends to the pub so riders have to go via the road from Higher Forston Farm, or send someone to fetch refreshments for them!

Go through the gate and bend right uphill on the grassy track to meet a gravel track. Turn left here. When the track divides at the head of a little copse, take the right hand fork up the hill and continue until you reach the road. *There are lovely views along this stretch.*

Further along the valley to the left is the well known village of Cerne Abbas with its chalk Giant.

On reaching the heavy, double, metal gates go through and onto the road (GR.678983). *Traffic here is light but can be fast.* Cross straight over the road and into an arable field keeping the roadside hedge on the right, head for the gap ahead leading into the next field. The bridleway goes across this vast field leaving a small copse up on the left to come to a metal waymarked gate in the hedge, but this may not be as shown on your Ordnance Survey Map. Go through this gate and turn right with the fence on the right, then turn left with the wire fence on the right and ride on headland to a small wicket gate in the corner. Go through this gate and carry on riding through the next field with the hedge on the right.

Go through a metal gate and ride straight ahead across an open arable field to meet a wide grass track coming in from the left (GR.692978). Ride ahead on this grass track, through the gate and follow the track right handed to a large metal gate that is waymarked. Here turn left into a wide grassy drove (GR.697974), ignore other bridleway signs, staying in the drove for about one mile. As the drove drops down to the village of White Lackington, it becomes metalled.

Continue past Lackington Farmhouse on the right and a track coming in on the left. Just after Riverway Cottage on the right go through a metal gate ahead and to the right of the village road (GR.709983). This is before Lambert Cottage on the left. Ride along this track which runs behind the village. Go through another metal gate with poplars on the left. After the next metal gate you are in a track. Turn right. After a few strides, take the left turn on the green lane that your ride started on, running behind

Piddlehinton. Continue back to Rectory Road and your starting point.

A 9 MILE CIRCULAR RIDE (CLOCKWISE)

Ordnance Survey Maps:
Landranger: 194
Pathfinder: 1317

Parking & Starting Point:
Parking is available at Orchard House, Toller Porcorum (GR.563982) by prior arrangement with Mr or Mrs Miller. Please telephone: 01300 320174. To find Orchard House, approach Toller Porcorum from the A356 down Toller Lane. At the start of the village there is a right turn by The Swan Inn. Turn right here into Kingcombe Road. On the right there are modern houses. Turn sharply to the right into the second driveway and follow it down to the stables. There is ample parking room here.

Route Description:

Ride out of the driveway and turn left into Kingcombe Road. At the T-junction turn right by The Swan Inn. Continue riding past the village and shop and telephone box on the right. The road bends left to cross the disused Bridport to Maiden Newton railway. *For 110 years there used to be a station in Toller Porcorum. Toller Porcorum means the Toller of the Pigs!*

Just after the railway bridge turn round the hairpin bend left into Frogmore Lane where there is a 'No Through Road' sign. Continue along this little lane which rises above the village. Where the lane ends at a property on the right, continue to ride straight ahead into a grassy lane with a sign 'Toller Fratrum 1 mile'.

At the bottom of this green lane, go through the gateway and turn right and then left over the stream, signed again to Toller Fratrum. Keep left up this field side and after a short distance go into a hedged lane and follow it for about 50 yards. Continue on through a waymarked gate and across the next field keeping the hedge on the right. Go through the waymarked gate in the corner of this field. From this gate, ride diagonally across the next field, leaving the little hill on your left. Drop down to a track in front of the hedge ahead which lies at the bottom of the hill. Bend left along the track to a gate in the corner of the narrow part of this field (GR.573974). Here the route crosses a tributary of the River Hooke.

Go through the left hand metal gate and ride up along the headland of this field with the hedge on the right. Ignore the first gate on the right and go through the second on the right which goes into a green lane which is hedged on both sides. After about 100 yards, you meet another track. Ride straight ahead keeping left on this track. This lane leads into the little hamlet of Toller Fratrum.

The 'Fratrum' or 'Brothers', were Knights of St John of Jerusalem, who owned the manor in medieval times. Little Toller Farm was built in the 1540's and the Church of St Basil was virtually rebuilt in the 19th Century. **Ride under the old aquaduct (GR.577973) and just before the hamlet, turn right. Go through the gate on the right, following the waymarker on a tree, and follow an obvious grassy track leading up to the left, with the hedge on the left. Stay on the track through the next gateway and continue climbing up**. *There is a good view of Toller Fratrum behind.* **In the field at the top, ride diagonally to the right across the field to a hunting gate which is in the hedge opposite.**

Manor, home of the Sydenham family, was rebuilt in 1630. **This is passed on the left by the T-junction. Turn right here and ride along the road for about 200 yards passing the farm (GR.583958). Where the road bends slightly right to go downhill, opposite the thatched cottage which is below in the field on the right, and where there is a stile in the fence on the right, go through the metal gate up on the left ahead. This leads to an obvious track with a hedge on the left and goes uphill.** *If you look back now it is possible to see the track you came along from Toller Fratrum to Wynford Eagle.*

Go through another metal gate and continue along the track which now bends left again, with the hedge on the left. *There are more lovely views all around here.* **After approximately 0.50 miles go through another gateway and on along a much**

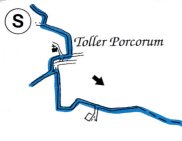

Toller Porcorum

Go through this waymarked hunting gate and continue to ride along the headland with the hedge on the left. Go through another gate and on to an obvious track crossing an open arable field to another gateway. Go through this and continue on the track with the wire fence now on the right. *The hamlet of Wynford Eagle is down to the left and ahead of you.*

Continue to ride down this track to the road, emerging opposite several cottages. Turn left and pass a little church (GR.581960). *This is the Church of St Lawrence, rebuilt in 1840, re-using the 15th century chancel arch from the earlier church. Set in the wall by the porch is a late 11th century tympanum, or head of the arch. The*

Little Toller Farm

Toller Fratrum

High Hill

Fore Hill Plantation

Trail 7

Wynford Eagle

narrower headland with the hedge on the left. At the end of this field go through the hunting gate which is in the left hand corner and turn right with wire fence on your right, continue to the next wooden hunting gate ahead. Go through this and ride diagonally across the field between the barn and the straggled trees to a hunting gate which is at the top of this field. *As several bridleways have been diverted in this area, the description given above may not match your Ordnance Survey Map.*

Go through the hunting gate and continue riding along the headland keeping the wire fence on the left. At the end of this field side, bend right inside the field and ride along with the roman road running parallel, just beyond the hedge on the left. Continue riding through two more fields going through the hunting gates. At the end of the second field, turn left through the field gate and onto the road. Continue riding along the road for 400 yards until the end of the roadside hedge on the right. Turn right into the field, leaving the hedge and hunting gate on the right and ride straight ahead away from the road onto a grass track which runs down across the field. *West Compton lies ahead in the valley.*

Go through a gate on to a steep hill and follow the little path with scrubby bushes to the right and a steep drop to the left. *Beware of rabbit holes here!* **Make your way**

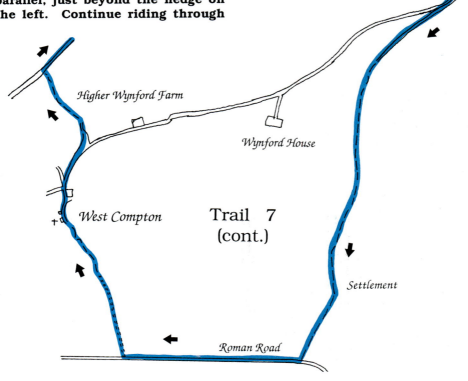

Wynford Eagle

Higher Wynford Farm

Wynford House

West Compton

Trail 7 (cont.)

Settlement

Roman Road

across this rough ground between gorse, brambles and scrub to go through a metal gate at the bottom. Continue through this small patch with ponds on the right. The track bends left going up a stony path and out on to a track which is in front of a large property which is now a holiday complex.

Turn right on this track and ride towards the hamlet of West Compton (GR.567937) and continue on until you meet the road. *The signpost here marks Bridport to the left, Maiden Newton to the right and Eggfarden Hill Farm straight ahead.*

Turn right. After a short distance, turn left off this road, where the telegraph poles change from the right side of the road to the left. Look carefully for this track; it is small and drops down beside trees and scrub into a wood. *It was used as a tip in the past and is still decorated with bits of freezers and fridges etc!* Ride through the stream. **Although the area through the wood can be a bit boggy, it is quite passable at the sides of the track.** Ahead of you there is a hunting gate in the corner - don't go through this. Instead, bend left, keeping the field hedge on the right to ride up the green lane which has a large hedge to either side. After about 100 yards the track comes out into an open field and is well waymarked.

When the hedge on the right turns right, continue riding straight ahead over an open field to a large gap in the hedge ahead. Go through the gap and continue on the headland with the hedge on the right. Emerge on to the road through the metal gate and turn right (GR.558953). *This is*

Shatcombe Lane and it is possible to park in the picnic area which lies 0.25 miles to the left.

Having turned right on the lane, continue to ride for about 0.25 miles and where the lane bends sharply right, carry on riding straight ahead on to an obvious track with a wire fence on the right and a hedge on the left until you come to a gate saying 'Ferndown' on it (GR.563957). *It is now possible to see Toller Porcorum ahead and the starting point of the ride.*

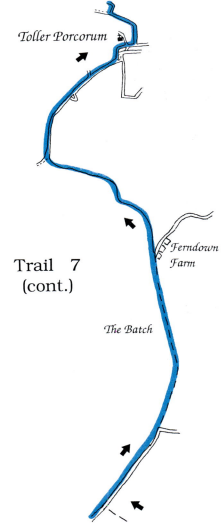

Toller Porcorum

Trail 7
(cont.)

Ferndown
Farm

The Batch

Continue riding for about 0.50 miles down this track and when the track goes into a farm, go through a metal gate which lies ahead on the left of the track. *The gate is signed Toller Porcorum 0.75 miles and waymarked with a red arrow. This is not marked on the Ordnance Survey map but it is a Council White road.*

Keep the hedge on the left and ride on into a lane which is hedged on both sides. When the hedges end, go straight on over the open field. There is a waymarker on the post in the field (GR.563970). Continue to ride on down the lane through the gorse to the little stream at the bottom and cross the bridge. Go through the metal gate and along the track which is now flanked by fir trees. At a junction of tracks, turn right up into a clearing and on to the village road. Turn right for Toller Porcorum and ride down the hill into the village, back over the disused railway and past the shop. Turn left by The Swan Inn into Kingcombe Road and turn right to your parking place by Orchard House.

St. Laurence Church
Wynford Eagle

THE BRITISH HORSE SOCIETY

BHS BOOK AND GIFT SHOP

The largest specialist Equestrian Bookshop in the UK displaying a comprehensive range of equestrian books and videos

The British Horse Society Book and Gift Shop is situated at the British Equestrian Centre on the Showground at Stoneleigh (on the B4113), and is open Monday to Saturday 9am-5pm. A full mail order service is available. Phone now for free catalogues.

Tel: 01203 690676

**BHS Book and Gift Shop
Stoneleigh Park, Kenilworth
Warwickshire CV8 2LR**

Registered Charity No 210504

The British Horse Society

A 7 MILE CIRCULAR TRAIL (ANTI-CLOCKWISE)

Ordnance Survey Maps:
Pathfinder: 1299
Landranger: 194

NB: *This ride can be extended to 9.5 miles and ridden as a figure of eight. Instructions are given at the end of the route directions.*

Parking & Starting Point:
Parking is available at Doles Ash (GR.716005). Please take care not to block any gateways or entrances. The route is described from Doles Ash Farm.

Route Description:

Opposite the entrance to Doles Ash Farm you will see a waymarked bridleway. Ride up this farm track with the hedge on the left and a field on the right. The track leads into another field with a hedge and trees on the right and an open field on the left. You are still following the farm track to this stage, but where it continues straight on through a scrubby piece of land with a wood on the left, turn left to keep the wood on the right. There is a waymarked bridleway here and the sign is in the brambles.

Continue on keeping the wood on the right following the waymarkers to the second corner of the wood. Here ride straight across the field at a slightly left diagonal to a waymarked hunting gate which is in the hedge. *You may have to look for this gate as it is set in the hedge.* **Go through this gate and turn immediately right to go through an iron gate. Ride along the top of the Down keeping the sheep fence on the right.** *This is a good place to canter if you wish.*

On reaching the wood, turn left, keeping the wood on the right. At the end of this wood, there is an iron gate on the right. Go through this and turn left. Ride along with the hedge and sheep fence on the left, towards a galvanized gate with a blue arrow marker. Go through this gate and follow the track along the ridge with the hedge and sheep fence on the left and the ground dropping steeply away on the right. *There are spectacular views along this stretch.*

Go through two hunt gates which are close together (GR.736027). When you are through the gates, look ahead and you will see a water trough in the middle of the field you are riding in. This trough is your goal, but to get there you have to ride around three sides of a large rectangle to achieve it! Continue riding with the hedge and down on your right, through a scrubby area into a large grassy field. Turn left, keeping the wire fence on your left. Go through the metal gate on the left and you are now facing a large water tank*.

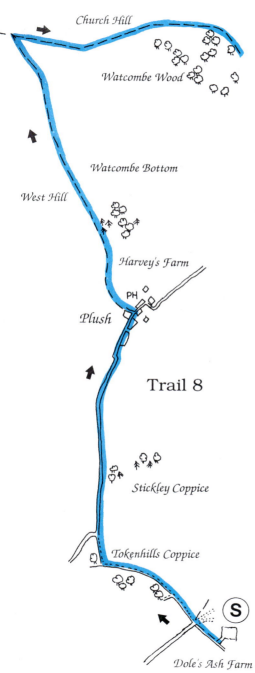

If you wish to ride in a figure of eight then follow the instructions given at the end of the ride from this point, otherwise continue as given below.

Ride to the water tank, then turn left and ride to the water trough you could see when you entered the field. Turn right at the trough and follow the grassy track down between the trees to a wooden gate. Go through this gate and ride on down the track with the wood on the right to meet another track coming in from the left. Keep right and carry on down the hill until you reach the road and go straight across. Follow the signpost to Alton Pancras **(GR.728033).** *At this point the ride has reached Folly Farmhouse, crossing the Plush to Mappowder road.*

Follow the waymarked track up the hill, through a gate and follow the track on to the Down. Ride through the gorse bushes and on up to a second gate, into a field keeping the hedge on the right. At the far corner of the field, go through another gate into the wood. Turn right and follow the track along the edge of the wood to a gateway where there is a map of the area, a waymark and the Wessex Ridgeway marker. Go through this gate and keeping the hedge on the right, ride half left across this long field toward the gate at the far end, through which you can see a barn. Do not go through this gate, but turn left instead **(GR.707036),** keeping the hedge on the right and you will see a waymarked gateway ahead. Go through this gap and ride along the Down on the faint track which lies above the deep bowl of Watcombe Bottom on the left.

From here you can just see Plush Church below, designed by Benjamin Ferrey in 1848. It has a 12th century font in the churchyard, all of which is sadly dilapidated.

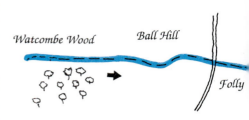

Watcombe Wood   Ball Hill

Folly

Head towards the corner of the wood which lies ahead, where you will come to a waymarked gate. Go through this and continue down the track keeping the wood on the left. Go through another gate and on down the track to another iron gate which opens on to the Piddletrenthide to Plush road (GR.714022).

Trail 8 (cont.)

Almost directly left of this gate is the well known Plush Public House, The Brace of Pheasants. This caters for both people and horses and there is a hitching rail at the back, albeit rather flimsy.

Turn right out of the gateway and ride for about 0.50 miles along the road. Where the road bends hard right, take the left turn on a stony track (GR.713009). Follow this track uphill for about one mile, passing a house on the right, to the top where the track emerges back at Doles Ash and your parking place.

Instructions for a figure of eight ride continue from here:

From the water trough (GR.736027) continue on to the large water tank ahead. Ride straight on the same line to a hunting gate (Wessex Ridgeway) and follow the track down to the woods. Go through the iron gate and take the left fork along a narrow path through the trees, emerging at the Dorset Gap (GR.744032). *Here you will find a green box, take out the book and sign your name!*

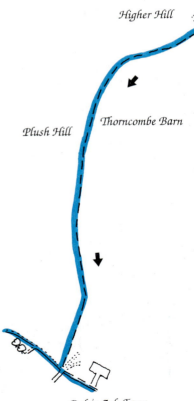

Higher Hill

Thorncombe Barn

Plush Hill

Dole's Ash Farm

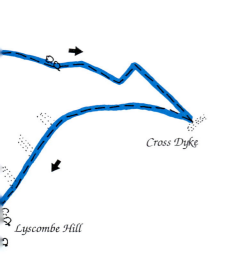

Cross Dyke

Lyscombe Hill

middle gate. Ride up to the top of the field, going straight on through a gate and over the ridge. Bear left and ride down the track. At the bottom, take the right hand gate of the two gates and go down the field with the hedge on the left, to the gate in the corner where five bridleways meet. Turn right here and ride on the road between Higher Melcombe Farm buildings and the big house.

Opposite the first farm cottage on the right, turn left signposted BW Lyscombe, and follow the track for 100 yards. Turn right through a hunting gate and follow the grass track to another hunt gate. Turn sharp left up the hill. At the top, keep straight on, going through double iron gates. Turn right and ride up the grassy track to the metal gate at the top. Go through this and head straight towards the large water tank in the middle of the field. Turn left and ride to the water trough (GR.736027) and, just before it, turn right into a grassy lane. Here you rejoin the instructions for the Plush Ride having completed your extra figure of eight loop.

Continue, leaving the green box on your left, to an iron gate leading on to a sunken grassy track on to Down Ridge. Ride on going through the next hunting gate and continue on keeping the wood on the left, until you reach three metal gates by the farm buildings. Here exit by the left hand gate and ride back through the

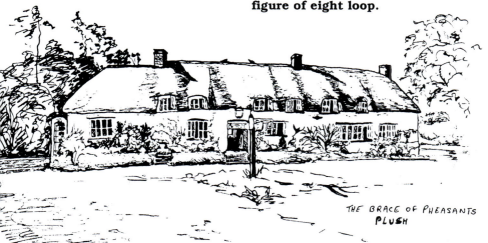

THE BRACE OF PHEASANTS
PLUSH

A 5 MILE CIRCULAR TRAIL (CLOCKWISE)

Ordnance Survey Maps:
Pathfinder: 1299
Landranger: 194

Parking & Starting Points:
Parking is available in the large car park at The Fox Inn, Ansty (GR.765033).

Route Description:

Turn left out of the Fox Inn car park and ride for approximately 0.75 miles through the villages of Ansty and Melcombe Bingham. Keep straight on at the first telephone box and the sign to Melcombe Park Farm and continue to a cross roads where there is another telephone box and a bus shelter on the left. Turn right here (GR.761023), signposted 'Private Road to Higher Melcombe'. Continue along this little road, with a big grassy verge and an avenue of trees on the left until you come to a cross roads of bridleways where two fir trees grow (GR.752025). Ride straight over and continue on to Higher Melcombe Farm, riding west on the tarmac farm road, keeping the big house on the left and farm buildings on the right. *To the right, you can see the humps and bumps of the site of the medieval settlement of Melcombe Horsey.*

Turn left opposite the first farm cottage on the right, on the bridleway signposted 'Lyscombe', and follow the track for about 100 yards. Turn sharp right through a hunting gate. Follow the grass track with the hedge on the right, and go through another hunt gate. Turn sharp left up the hill, with the hedge on the left. This becomes a farm track on a shallow sunken road. *As you ride up the hill there is a marvellous view from here.* At the top of the hill (GR.743021), keep straight on, going through double iron gates. Turn sharp right and ride up the grass keeping the sheep fence and wood on the right. *This is a good place for a nice long canter. Spectacular views of the Dorset countryside are on the left. On a clear day it is possible to see Hardy's Monument.*

Keep going up the grassy track, through the gap in the gorse to the top. Here there is a wire fence. Go through an iron gate in the corner

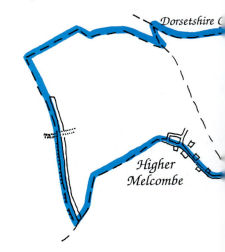

Dorsetshire (

Higher Melcombe

and ride straight on towards a large water tank 300 yards ahead. **Turn sharp right at the tank and ride in a straight line down the middle of the field .** *Ahead on the horizon are the two Bulbarrow Radio Masts.* **Go through the hunting gate and follow the sunken track down the hill to the woods. Go through the iron gate and take the left hand fork in the track, signposted 'Bridleway Dorset Gap'. This narrow track winds through the trees on the side of the hill and into a deep cutting. At the bottom is a signpost on the crossroads of tracks. You are now in the middle of the Dorset Gap (GR.744032).**

Here, in the midst of the Dorset countryside, you will find a green box. If you wish, dismount and lift the lid of the box, take out the book and sign your

name, perhaps giving a little explanation for your visit. **Leaving the box on the left, take the track signposted Melcombe Bingham which goes up through an iron gate marked with a Wessex Ridgeway sign. Keep going up the grassy, sunken track bearing left along the ridge.** *There are marvellous views in all directions, with the Blackmore Vale to the left. Also, many chalk loving wild flowers grow here in the spring and summer.*

Go through a hunt gate and continue down the field, keeping alongside the woods on the left. Head for the farm buildings of Melcombe Park Farm (GR.751034). In the corner you will see three gates next to each other. Go through the left hand gate and then straight on into the yard, leaving the barns on the left and a modern house on the right. Continue on down this small road, following round to the right at the wood. Continue to Ansty and when you reach the road turn left, to finish your ride at the Fox Inn.

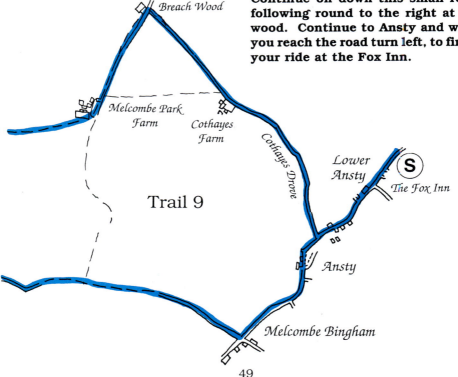

A 12.5 MILE CIRCULAR TRAIL (ANTI-CLOCKWISE)

Ordnance Survey Maps:
Pathfinder: 1317
Landranger: 194

Parking & Starting Points:
Parking is available on the large, grassy area by the side of the road in Shatcombe Lane by Eggardon Hill (GR.550948). Your route is described from the picnic area here.

Route Description:

Leave your parking place and turn right on to the road, then left at the T-junction and right at the next crossroads. *The road work just described is all within sight of your parking place. Eggardon Hill is now on the left. This ancient hill fort is 800 feet above sea level and when you return at the end of the ride, a Celtic Field system can be seen on the south-east side.*

Follow the small road for about 1.50 miles down to Kings Farm and Whetley Farm (GR.532963). Go past Whetley Farm and turn right after the left hand bend, signed 'Stones Common'. Go through the gate, on to a track past houses and out through another gate into a field. Ride across the field keeping straight ahead to a hunting gate leading into Powerstock Common.

Powerstock Common was a Royal Forest in 1201. Recently planted with spruce,

Loscombe Farm

Marlpits Farm

Leigh Gate

West Milton

pine and beech, by the Forestry Commission, it is now leased by the Dorset Trust for Nature Conservation. Under their management, it is reverting to natural habitat, with areas cleared for many species of butterflies, insects, birds and snakes.

Continue after the gate, until the path in the clearing forks. Keep straight ahead, going up past Dorset Trust and WWF signs, on a rough path through trees. Further up, you will come to a T-junction of paths, stay right handed - not left, onto the visible hard forestry track. Continue straight on, past the waymarked bridleway on the right, until you reach the main forestry track. Ride

straight over, staying to the right of the bridged footpath area. *You will pass a recently uncovered kiln.*

Continue riding through a clearing, keeping right handed, to join the main track. Turn left here (GR.547974) to come to a road. Turn left, go under the bridge, and ride for about 2.25 miles on a small, quiet and attractive road. Ignore the right turn which is opposite a farm track

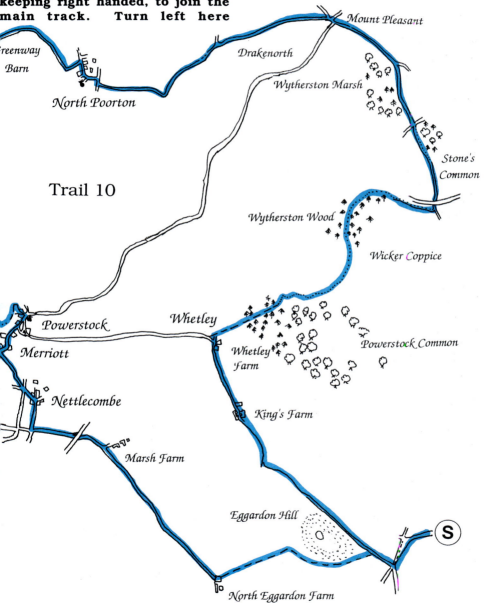

on the left. Stay left at the next junction. After a mile from the bridge, you will reach Mount Pleasant Cross roads, with fir trees (GR.538987). Here, take the second turn left to North Poorton. Stay left at the next junction and continue on down the hill to the T-junction at the bottom. Turn right here down a 'No Through Road', signed to North Poorton and Burcombe only. Turn almost immediately first left on a hard track past thatched cottages and a church on the left and a farm on the right. Bend round to the left after the farm, where another track goes right.

Continue riding on the concrete track which later becomes an unmade surface, then grassy winding down the hill to Loscombe which lies at the bottom (GR.503979). Continue riding through the small hamlet of Loscombe to a T-junction. Turn left here into the usually dry ford and follow the road up the hill to a cross roads at the top. Ride straight over to Leigh Gate. Here you will come to a farm with horses. Between the bungalow and farm, hidden between bushes and a slatted wooden fence, you will find a small bridleway which takes you steeply down an old sunken track to the village of West Milton (GR.503964). At the bottom, continue slightly uphill, ignoring another inviting sunken lane on the left. Stay on the metalled lane, passing cottages on either side.

Before you reach the church, there is a decision to be made; the choice is between riding for a mile along a small road with some traffic; or a mile of typically difficult West Dorset bridleway!

If you choose the road: continue past the church on the left, on down the road to the bottom. At the signpost, telephone box and bus shelter, turn left. Go over the bridge and turn left again, signed 'Powerstock 1 mile, Nettlecombe 1.25 miles'. Continue straight on at the road junction where the Powerstock road comes in from the left, to meet the Marquis of Lorne public house at the beginning of Nettlecombe.

If you choose the bridleway - it's not that bad really!: Turn left before the church, signed Ridgeback Lane, and go through Church Farm. After the farmyard, go through the gate and straight on up a green lane for 50 yards. Turn right through two gates into a field. Keep the hedge on the right and go down the field to two small gates at the bottom. *It is suggested here that one rider dismounts and opens the gates which can be awkward.* Turn left over the bridge which can be slippery when it is wet, into a narrow track. This track leads to a field which is very rough. Continue riding in a straight line, even when the track goes up to the left: keep the stream down to the right. There may be electric fencing alongside just here. At the narrowing of the field, go through a waymarked bridle gate into a lane. This track continues straight on and then turns left when you reach Powerstock, where you come out above a large chapel-like building.

Keeping this building on the right, continue to a road. *If you are in need of refreshment now, continue straight across at the crossroads to The Three Horseshoes which is to be found on the right.*

Otherwise, turn right at the cross roads (GR.516964), signposted 'West Milton, Bridport'. Follow this road to Nettlecombe, turning left at the T-junction out of Powerstock. Take the left fork at The Marquis of Lorne public house in Nettlecombe. Continue riding through the village, ignoring the 'No Through Road' to the left, to a T-junction (GR.517954). Turn left here and continue under the railway bridge. Keep right at the triangle signed 'Bridleway Spyway 1.5, North Eggardon Farm, No Through Road'. Continue to North Eggardon Farm. When you reach the farm buildings (GR.534943), go sharp left and follow the signed bridleway up on to Eggardon Hill. Keep right around the grassy moat to a field gate. Go through this gate and through the bridleway gate immediately opposite and follow the bridleway across a field. This will bring you out on the small road your ride started on. Turn right, then left and then right to arrive back at your parking place.

CRANBORNE SQUARE

A 5.75 MILE CIRCULAR TRAIL (ANTI-CLOCKWISE)

Ordnance Survey Maps:
Pathfinder: 1317
Landranger: 193 & 194

Parking & Starting Point:
Parking is available by prior arrangement with Mr & Mrs Newall at Mapperton Farm (GR.496994). Please telephone 01308 862250. Your route is described from this point.

Route Description:

Turn left out of Mapperton Farm. Pass the Posy Tree on the left. *The Posy Tree dates back from the plague and the notice on the tree gives details.* **Take the second waymarked bridleway on the right, almost opposite the cottages. Go across the field leaving Mapperton Manor on the left. Turn right on the tarmac track and go through the field gate, leaving the cottage on the right. Follow the grassy track down the combe, leaving the gardens up on the left. Go through a field gate at the bottom on the right and follow the sandy track with the wood on the right.**

Where the track bends left by a large tree, take the right handed lower track to the wood, leaving the remains of Smugglers Cottage on the left. Go through a gate into the wood, proceed over the ford and out of the wood through another gate. Here a track comes in from the left

and your route goes right, through a gateway and continues to Loscombe Farm. Go through the farmyard and keep right handed on a sandy track leading into a sunken lane, to emerge on a small road in Loscombe. On the right there is a house with a conservatory (GR.502979).

Turn left here and follow the track uphill. After 0.75 miles, the grassy track becomes a concrete farm track. Continue, bending round to the left. Another track comes in from the left but you keep right here, leaving the farm buildings on the left and the thatched cottages and church on the right. *This is the parish of North Poorton.* **When you reach the T-junction (GR.520982), turn left and follow the small 'No Through Road' to Burcombe.**

Ignore the waymarked bridleway to the right and continue to the end of the road. At Burcombe Cottage (GR.518987), turn right through a field gate and follow the track left handed to the top of the hill. Here go half right diagonally across a field, keeping the hedge to the right. Follow the hedge round a corner and go through a field gate into a track. *This leads down over a stream and along a lovely valley, recently resurfaced with sandstones.*

After the next field gate (GR.513993), turn steeply right, up a grassy bank alongside a resurfaced track. Go through the gate into a

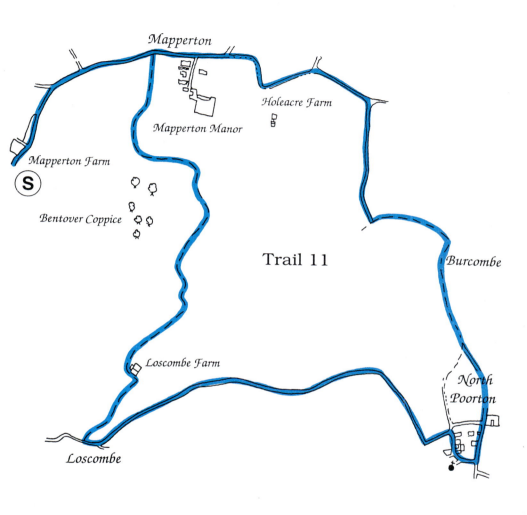

Mapperton

Holeacre Farm

Mapperton Manor

Mapperton Farm

(S)

Bentover Coppice

Trail 11

Burcombe

Loscombe Farm

North Poorton

Loscombe

lane and at the top, turn left (GR.512998). Follow this hard track and keep straight on where it joins the road, leaving Mapperton Manor on the left. You will rejoin your starting point at Mapperton Farm on the right.

A 10 MILE CIRCULAR TRAIL (CLOCKWISE)

Ordnance Survey Maps:
Pathfinders: 1317 & 1331
Landranger: 194

Parking & Starting Point:
Parking is available by prior arrangement with Jane Dowling at Whatcombe House, Little Bredy (GR.578897). Telephone 01308 482275.

Route Description:

From the driveway of Whatcombe House, turn left on to the road and ride for about 0.75 miles on this small road into the village of Little Bredy which lies at the head of the Bride Valley. When you reach the village, keep straight on, leaving the octagonal wooden bus shelter on the right. At the fork in the road, by the telephone box, with barns on both the left and right hand side, take the right hand fork down a lesser road (GR.589890).

On the right is Bridehead House, built in 1837. **Turn right through a metal gate signed 'Landowners welcome caring riders'.** *The cricket pavilion is on the left and there is a good view of the house on the right.* **Keep straight on the track at the side of the cricket field to another metal gate with a stile on the left. After this gate, the main track goes right handed, but the route follows the grassy track**

straight ahead, up through a few trees and bears round to the left. Follow the grass track towards the woods in front, with a lovely wooded valley down to the left.

When you reach the wood, continue on keeping the wood close to the left even when the track peters out, until you come to a stone barn with a gate on the left (GR.591878). *NB. This barn has been granted permission for development.* **Go through this metal gate and leave the barn on the left. Stay right, ignoring the lane to the left, keeping the wire fence on the left, to go up a stony track with grass growing in the middle.**

Continue along this track for some way, with wire fences on either side. *At this point you can see Hardy's Monument to your left.* **Continue on the track, now hedged on the left, passing a corrugated iron building on the right.**

From this spot you have a panoramic view of West Dorset to the right and, on a clear day you can see West Bay, Bridport and the hills beyond. Also coming into view on the left, and in front, is the sea and a stunning view of Chesil Bank and the Fleet, and Portland Island and Weymouth. **At the end of this track, when it becomes metalled and stony, you meet a hedge (GR.588867).** *To the right there is a sign saying 'Kingston Russell Stone Circle', which is part of the Hardy's Monument Ride.*

Long Bredy

Manor Farm   Whatcombe Down

(S)   Whatcombe House

Long Bredy Farm   Pitcombe Down

Knapp Farm   Littlebredy

Bridehead

Trail 12

Chapel Coppice   Ashley Dairy

Abbotsbury Castle   Wears Farm   White Hill

SWC Path

Go left here, down a stony track where almost immediately you will meet a farm track. Continue to the road where there is a small grassy triangle. Turn sharp right here and continue for 100 yards to the corner where the road bends left (GR.587866). Go straight ahead here through a hunting gate to the right of a field gate. A wooden sign says 'West Bexington 3 1/2 miles'. Keeping the fence on the left, continue to a wooden sign post in the fence on the left. Turn right here signed 'Inland Route West Bexington'. Continue riding straight on through what is usually a cultivated patch, with fir wood over to the right and the sea on the left. Ride for nearly two miles on this line with the sea to the left.

From this point you can see St Catherines Chapel perched on the top of Chapel Hill to the left above the sea. This chapel was built in the late 14th century and survived the dissolution of the monasteries because it was useful as a sea mark. Legend has it that spinsters could pray here for a husband on a certain day in the year.

You are now riding along White Hill, through gateways on the obvious track with wooden signs and waymarks. *This is a good place for a canter if you wish, whilst enjoying the lovely views.*

When you reach a grassy divide to the field and a concrete water trough, go through the field gate on the left with a stile to the left of the gate. Keep the wire fence on the right. There is a sign here reading 'Abbotsbury' to the left, 'Hill Fort and West Bexington' straight ahead. *Now*

is an opportunity to visit Abbotsbury, which is a pretty village with a pub, a few shops and a blacksmith's forge with a working blacksmith. Abbotsbury is also famous for the sub-tropical gardens to the west and the Swannery, home to mute swans since at least the 14th century. Both these venues are better visited without your horse! Also worth a visit is the huge barn, near to the Swannery. Originally 270 feet long and built about 1400, it is one of the largest in England.

Continue your ride through the next metal gate with a stile on the right, into a narrower grassy strip which is another good place for a long canter if you wish. You are now riding along West Hill, which brings you into a long field with two hummocks in front of you. The right hand hummock has a structure on top, and the route lies between the two hummocks. Stay along the top of this downland, passing telegraph poles and a farm down to the right. There are gorse bushes either side and a steep hill down to the left leading to the sea. Continue along the top - the main road from Abbotsbury to Bridport comes into view here.

When you reach the end of this stretch of downland, there is a stile on to the road (GR.557864). This should be the bridleway gate, but if the gate is not yet in place, keep right, up a little chalky incline and along the side of the boundary fence to a gate in the corner, leading out on to a minor road. Turn right on the road, and continue to the top of the hill. Here take the grassy fork off to the left. Continue along this track, passing a cylindrical water store on the left, scrubby trees on either side of the track and the edge of Ashley Chase on the right. After approximately 0.50 miles, you will see a pillbox type water tank, covered in vegetation. Go beyond the pillbox and take the first metal field gate on the right (GR.555883). Go through this and ride straight on with the wire fence on the right, through the next field gate and follow the indented cart track between the two woods, downhill.

At the bottom of this field adjoining the right hand wood, is another gate. Go through this gate on to a concrete farm track, still going downhill. Continue through the farmyard, bending right to leave the dilapidated farmhouse on the right. When you reach a lane, turn left and continue up the hill, ignoring the track to the left. At the top, the route bends round to the right. When you reach a rather messy cross track area (GR.567883), turn left into a farm track which is hedged on both sides. This obvious track takes you all the way down to the valley for over a mile. *You can see Whatcombe House where your ride started.*

At the farmyard, the track becomes tarmaced. Keep straight on here towards the village of Long Bredy. Ride over a bridge, with a small stream on the right. Pass the rather fine looking Kingston Russell House on the right. *Kingston Russell House was built in the late 17th and early 18th century.* Keep straight on where a more major road comes in from the left. Turn first right signed to Little Bredy 1 3/4 miles and Dorchester 9 miles. Continue along this road for 0.75 miles when you will find Whatcombe House up on the left and your starting point.

ST. CATHERINES CHAPEL

A 7 MILE CIRCULAR TRAIL (CLOCKWISE)

Ordnance Survey Maps:
Pathfinders: 1317, 1331 & 1332
Landranger: 194

Parking & Starting Point:
Parking is available by prior arrangement with Jane Dowling at Whatcombe House, Little Bredy (GR.578897). Telephone 01308 482275.

Route Description:

From Whatcombe House, turn right and ride for a few hundred yards along the road to turn right through a metal gate leading onto a chalky track which takes you up the hill. Follow this track through gateways uphill, ignoring a right fork. At the very top of the hill you meet a triangle of fencing and gates (GR.579905). Go through the gate ahead of you and into the triangle and turn right out through another gate, keeping the fence on the right and ride on through two fields.

From the next large field you can see Hardy's Monument ahead of you. **DO NOT BE TEMPTED TO CANTER HERE:** *the downland has been ploughed in the past and the grassland is now flinty.* **Go straight across the middle of this field, past a fenced tumulus on the left and through the double gate in front of you into a grassy lane. Keep in the lane with a hedge on the right**

and wire on the left, with wooded areas down to the left. Continue through a field gate, still heading for the distant Hardy's Monument. At the end of this track you meet the cross roads with a triangle of grass (GR.596893).

Continue riding straight ahead for about 0.50 miles on the road signed to Portisham and Abbotsbury - the Monument is now ahead on the left. Another road comes up from the right, but you keep on the higher road and continue slightly uphill with the wooded area now on the left. When you come to an area of scrub (GR.600884), take one of the grassy paths off to the left, before the electricity lines. The first path emerges on a track where you bend left and continue to a fork in the path. On the right is a small information sign. Turn right here, keeping open fields on the left and woodland on the right. When you reach the Portisham road, cross straight over.

Continue along this track for about 0.25 miles. It leads into a wood and when you reach a small clearing in the wood, take a single path going off to the right, uphill, away from the more inviting grassy way ahead. Follow this track for some way through the wood, until it rejoins the main track, coming in from the left. Turn right and continue until you arrive at the road (GR.616878). Now turn either right on the road and ride

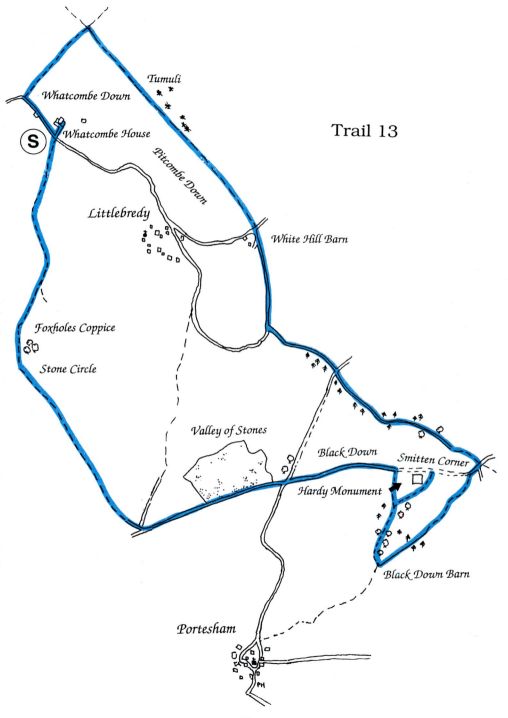

Trail 13

S

Whatcombe Down

Tumuli

Whatcombe House

Pitcombe Down

Littlebredy

White Hill Barn

Foxholes Coppice

Stone Circle

Valley of Stones

Black Down

Smitten Corner

Hardy Monument

Black Down Barn

Portesham

PH

up to Hardy's Monument (GR.613876), or shortly after turning right on the road, take a bridleway on the left to ride a circuit of the woods below the Monument.

For the latter, follow the bridleway on the left until it meets a main track. Turn right and continue on the main track, ignoring other paths on either side, until there is a fork with a grassy track going right. Keep right here until you meet another track coming in from the left. Turn right again and follow this path uphill, keeping straight on at a crossing where the sign post says 'Hardy's Monument 1/4 mile'. *When you reach the Monument, take time to admire the view; on a fine day you can see the Devon coastline and Bulbarrow to the north. The Monument commemorates the life of Admiral Sir Thomas Hardy 1769-1839, hero of Trafalgar and Nelson's 'kiss me Hardy' fame.*

Ride back on to the road and turn left. There is now about 1.50 miles of road work. Cross over the Portisham road and continue straight ahead on the little road marked: Gorwell 2 miles. When you reach a fork in the road with a grassy triangle (GR.589867), turn right: the wooden signpost says 'Bridleway Kingston Russell 3 1/2 miles'.

On reaching a gate and cattle grid where there is a Caravan Club sign, keep right and go straight on through a hunting gate beside a field gate with a sign to Stone Circle. Continue through three fields with a hedge on the left. *To the left in this area is The Grey Mare and her Colts - a Neolithic long barrow whose large Sarsen stones are now exposed. In the*

early 19th century, the barrow was opened and human bones were found. Long barrows were communal graves.

When you reach the fourth field, turn right, leaving the stone circle on the left (GR.577877). *This circle probably dates from the Bronze Age - about 4000 years ago. It is a very small scale and simple version of Stonehenge.*

Continue along the headland leaving the spinney on the right, to a wire fence ahead. Go left here and continue to a gate in the wire fence on the right. Go through this into a large field. Ride straight ahead over the brow of this hill and drop steeply down. The wood on the right gets closer as you descend, and you head for a gate in the far right corner, where the field becomes much narrower towards the wood. *From here, you can look across to Whatcombe House where your ride started.*

Go through the gate and ride diagonally across the length of this field, with a narrow belt of woodland on your right. At the furthest diagonal corner, you will see a gate with vertical bars. Go through this gate and continue down through a reedy field to the bottom. Go through the next gate and across the field, riding over a concrete bridge over the stream and through another gate with vertical bars. Continue up the next field with the hedge on the right, towards Whatcombe House, and through two metal gates on to the road. The driveway to Whatcombe House is immediately in front of you.

CRANBORNE CHASE

Cranborne Chase is a large area of chalk downland surrounded by wooded river valleys, mainly in North East Dorset. Since Saxon times it was a royal hunting ground and only the Lord of the Chase was allowed to kill the deer, and their woodlands were preserved until 1838, by law. This title was held by the Monarchy from William the Conqueror to James I who granted it to Cecil, later Earl of Salisbury. It was later sold to Lord Shaftesbury and lastly to the Pitt-Rivers family from Tollard Royal.

Several great manor houses and hunting lodges were built to accommodate the royal visitors.

The Chase is designated as an Area of Outstanding Natural Beauty and contains many prehistoric barrows and Roman remains. Several rides link up with the ancient Wessex Ridgeway and Roman Ackling Dyke.

Ashmore is the highest village in the Chase. There are many attractive stone cottages surrounding the village pond. The pond is very old; it was certainly known to the Romans and is probably of earlier origin. It is deeper than it seems, being 16ft deep in the middle. The well-kept church has unexpected 20th century corbels depicting animals of the Chase. Manor Farmhouse, near

the church, has a band of corbelling which probably came from nearby Eastbury House when it was demolished.

The path from Stubhampton Bottom to Washer's Pit passes close to West Lodge, the best preserved of the Chase lodges.

It is thought that the prosperity brought to Tarrant Gunville was probably due to Eastbury House. There is a greater elegance about the houses here than elsewhere in the valley - an impression heightened by the fine, mature trees. On the hillside of Everley Hill lies the church. Reset outside on the south wall of the chancel is an unusual monument stone to the parson of 1567. The church is better viewed from the outside. The interior is large and does not have a sense of harmony that is present in the other valley churches.

Below the church is the Old Rectory built in 1798, a substantial three-storey building. Gunville Manor and its stable block with little cupola, stands above the churchyard and forms an attractive backdrop to the impressive array of gravestones. This was built about the same time as the Old Rectory.

A 12 MILE CIRCULAR RIDE (CLOCKWISE)

Ordnance Survey Maps:
Pathfinder: 1281
Landranger: 184 & 195

Parking & Starting Point:
There is limited parking available at Stubhampton Bottom (GR.914142), on the wide grass verge on the right hand side under the bridleway sign to Washers Pit. This is by the well marked bend on the Tarrant Hinton to Iwerne Minster Road. Parking is also available by prior arrangement with Mr & Mrs Goswell at the Bugle Horn in Tarrant Gunville. Telephone 01258 830300. They can also provide a packed lunch if ordered in advance. If you park here you will need to ride just over one mile up through the village to the start of the described route.

Of Interest:
Ashmore is the highest, and probably the oldest, village in Dorset still on its original pre-Roman site. It is set round a large pond with many ducks and geese, and lovely old stone houses, several of them thatched. On the rare occasions that the pond dried out, last in 1911, the ancient custom was to hold a feast, then farmers were allowed to dig out the rich mud to spread on their fields.

Route Description:

1. Follow the signpost through the main woodland track of Stubhampton Bottom until you meet the road to Washers Pit (GR.898168). *This valley is well known for its large variety of wild flowers, butterflies and trees.*

2. Cross the road to the left hand side and turn right into Fontmell Woods to follow the main bridleway, turning left at the top opposite a field. Go through a beech avenue and then turn right at a T-junction (GR.889178) to a gate on to the road. *There is good visibility here, but traffic may be fast.* There are fine views over Fontmell Down to Blackmore Vale. **Turn right onto the grass verge and then turn right again in 0.33 miles to ride past Compton Abbas Airfield.** *Beware here of small private planes taking off and landing on the other side of the hedge.*

Ride for 0.33 miles to take the bridleway on the right (GR.895186). Go through the gate followed by several more gates, via Shepherd's Bottom, to emerge to the right of Manor Farm. Turn left.

3. *It is well worth going past the church for a short distance to see the village pond. This is a good place to give your horse a drink.* **Return to the bridleway on the left (GR.911176). This bridleway is also marked with the Wessex Wyvern as it is the start of the Dorset section of the Ridgeway.** *This may differ from that shown on your Ordnance Survey map.* **Ride into the woods and turn left riding**

on until you reach **Well Bottom (GR.917165).** *In May the woods are full of bluebells.*

4. Keep to the right round the forestry trail and ride down the wood track for 0.50 miles, going through a gate, following the grassy valley down through Ashmore Bottom past a modern farm to Stubhampton where your starting place is on the right with The Bugle Horn public house along the lane to the left.

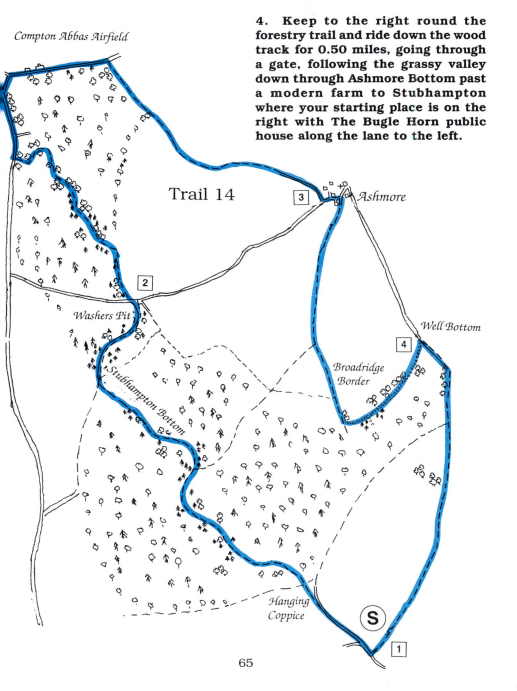

Compton Abbas Airfield

Trail 14

3

Ashmore

2

Washers Pit

Well Bottom

4

Stubhampton Bottom

Broadridge Border

Hanging Coppice

S

1

TARRANT GUNVILLE, HARBINS PARK & CHETTLE

TRAIL 15

AN 11 MILE CIRCULAR RIDE (CLOCKWISE)

Ordnance Survey Maps:
Pathfinder: 1281
Landranger: 195

Parking & Starting Point:
Parking is available by prior arrangement with Mr & Mrs Goswell at The Bugle Horn, Tarrant Gunville. Telephone 01258 830300. (GR.927127)

Of Interest:
Opposite The Bugle Horn are the grounds of Eastbury House which was designed by Sir John Vanbrugh as a magnificent mansion, taking 20 years to build. By the time it was finished in 1738, the owner had died and left it to his nephew, George Bubb Dodington, but when the family could not afford the upkeep, some 30 years later, it was demolished, except for one remaining wing and a Roman arch with two pine trees sprouting on the top.

This ride also goes through the park of Chettle House which lies 2 miles to the east of Eastbury. It is a lovely Queen Anne mansion designed and built, in 1710 for the Chafin family. This house with mellowed brickwork with rounded corners and stone dressings should be admired from a distance, in the garden. When the last member died in 1818 there were legal disputes and it became neglected until the Castlemans restored it in 1846. Chettle House is now divided into flats and open to the public.

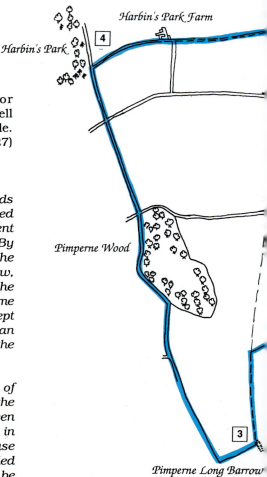

Harbin's Park Farm

Harbin's Park

4

Pimperne Wood

3

Pimperne Long Barrow

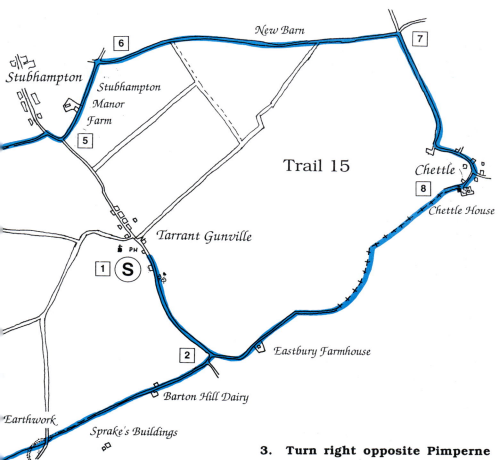

New Barn

Stubhampton

Stubhampton
Manor
Farm

Trail 15

Chettle

Chettle House

Tarrant Gunville

S

Eastbury Farmhouse

Barton Hill Dairy

Earthwork

Sprake's Buildings

Route Description:

1. From the public house in Tarrant Gunville, turn right and ride for 0.50 miles and on the second of the double bends, turn right (GR.932120).

2. Follow this lane past Barton Hill Dairy up to a hedge. Turn left then diagonally right following the bridleway signs between fields, ignoring a private gravel track. *This may differ from that shown on your Ordnance Survey Map.*

3. Turn right opposite Pimperne Long Barrow (GR.917105) going through a narrow gateway in the hedge to turn right again just past two old walls. Ride straight on for almost two miles. *There is a good place to canter if you wish, on the wide grass verge passing Pimperne Woods.* **Cross a track, then fields and a road to come to Harbin's Park.**

Harbin caused great aggravation to the Lord of the Chase by tempting the deer to jump into his private park for apple pulp left from cider making. However, because of a ditch on the inner side of the park, the deer were unable to jump out again!

4. Turn right (GR.905130) and ride down the verges to Harbin's Park Farm and ride straight on through a gate and fields until you meet the Stubhampton road. Turn right.

5. Ride along the road, then turn left where the signpost reads Bussey Stool (GR.921134).

6. At the Eastbury Estate crossroads take the grass bridleway track on the right (GR.923139). *This is another place to enjoy a canter if you wish.* Follow the lane for 1.50 miles, past a barn, until you come to a giant chestnut tree on a junction (GR.946144).

7. Turn right and ride down the road which winds through Chettle, forking right twice past the church to come to the park gates (GR.950132).

8. *If you divert 50 yards down the bridleway here, there are splendid views of Chettle House and gardens to the left.*

Return to the park gates and follow the red byway arrow across the open park and through the double gates at the top. Keep left round the woods, leaving a bridleway track on your right and stay on the byway between open fields, passing Eastbury Farmhouse. Turn right (GR.932120) and ride back to The Bugle Horn.

TARRANT RAWSTON
CHURCH

Fairfield Country House Hotel
Accommodation & Restaurant
For you and your horse, with local grazing

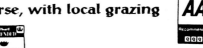

Fully operational
disabled suite

Traditional
Sunday lunches

Evening a la carte
menu (Tues -Sat)

Superb, modern
en-suite facilities

Ample car park
& garden

Comfortable open-
fire lounge bar

Dorset cream teas

Church Road, Pimperne, Nr Blandford.
Tel: (01258) 456756
Proprietors: Alan & Frances Bromley

BADBURY RING, ACKLING DYKE & TARRANT MONKTON

A 12 MILE CIRCULAR TRAIL (ANTI-CLOCKWISE)

Ordnance Survey Maps:
Pathfinder: 1300
Landranger: 195

Parking & Starting Points:
Parking is available in the large National Trust Car Park (GR.963033). Badbury Rings is 3 miles west of Wimborne on the B3082 road to Blandford.

Of Interest:
The approach to Badbury Rings is along a magnificent avenue of beech trees linking the Rings to Kingston Lacy House, which is well worth visiting. Badbury Rings is an Iron Age hill fort constructed in about 500 BC. The impressive clump of trees is surrounded by three defensive lines of ramparts and ditches.

Each Spring several local hunts hold point-to-point races around the fields on the west slopes.

In about 43 AD the Romans drove out the local Durotriges and made this fort the centre of a new network of roads extending to the Port of Hamworthy, Bath, Dorchester and Old Sarum. This ride uses part of this last Roman road, running north, called the Ackling Dyke. Further information can be found on the notice boards that have been erected by the National Trust.

It is worthwhile to make the two mile diversion to Tarrant Monkton for refreshments, fording the River Tarrant beside a packhorse bridge, passing pretty thatched cottages on a quiet lane to the Langton Arms public house.

Route Description:

1. Ride down the slope at the north west corner of the Rings and up the bridleway past the Oaks, to join the Ackling Dyke, first on a gravel track then a grass lane. Ride for about 1.50 miles to meet a junction of three roads (GR.977058).

2. Turn left before Zannies Cottages and go straight over the crossroads. Turn left onto the bridleway (GR.979068) by two large trees. *Enjoy a canter here if you wish.* **Bear right at Birch Coppice. After one mile you will pass several cottages and meet a tarmac road (GR.978078).**

3. Cross over on to a grass path which bears right at Manswood and cross again up a farm lane, bearing left past a bench and into the woodland, keeping right to Cockroad Farm. Turn left and then at a fork in the road, right to a road bend (GR.976092).

4. Go straight over and follow the field edge right, then left for 0.50 miles to a T-junction (GR.968096). *There are lovely views here from Horse Down where the Marten family keep the bridleways in such good condition on their Crichel Estate.*

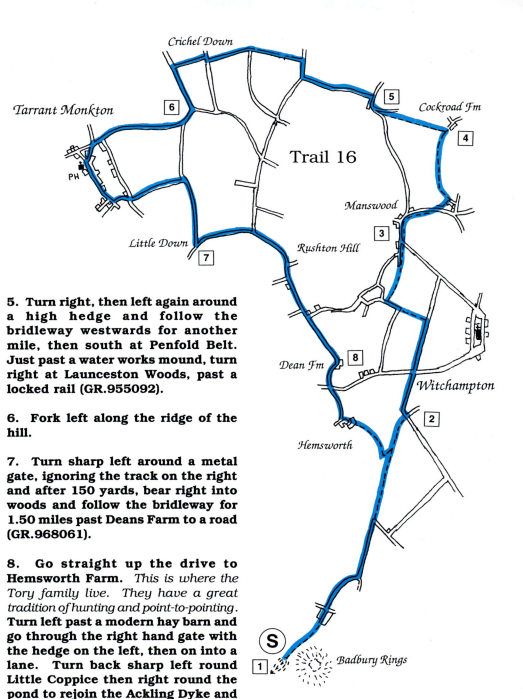

Crichel Down

Tarrant Monkton

6

PH

Little Down

7

Trail 16

5

Cockroad Fm

4

Manswood

3

Rushton Hill

Dean Fm 8

Witchampton

2

Hemsworth

1

S

Badbury Rings

5. Turn right, then left again around a high hedge and follow the bridleway westwards for another mile, then south at Penfold Belt. Just past a water works mound, turn right at Launceston Woods, past a locked rail (GR.955092).

6. Fork left along the ridge of the hill.

7. Turn sharp left around a metal gate, ignoring the track on the right and after 150 yards, bear right into woods and follow the bridleway for 1.50 miles past Deans Farm to a road (GR.968061).

8. Go straight up the drive to Hemsworth Farm. *This is where the Tory family live. They have a great tradition of hunting and point-to-pointing.* **Turn left past a modern hay barn and go through the right hand gate with the hedge on the left, then on into a lane. Turn back sharp left round Little Coppice then right round the pond to rejoin the Ackling Dyke and retrace your steps back to Badbury Rings and your parking place.**

NB. *If you wish to visit Tarrant Monkton when you reach 6. in the route description, fork right down Turners Lane and ride for a short distance down the road ahead to the ford. Wade through the clear Tarrant chalk stream, noting the ancient packhorse bridge. Keep left between the thatched cottages to the Langton Arms where you can take refreshment.*

Wind south through the village and cros. carefully past the signpost up Commo. Drove to join the route southwards on wide grass path on the right to Stubb. Coppice (GR.956078). Continue at 7. i. route description.

NORTH POORTON

BOTTLEBUSH DOWN, GUSSAGE ALL SAINTS, ACKLING DYKE

TRAIL 17

A 10 MILE CIRCULAR TRAIL (CLOCKWISE)

Ordnance Survey Maps:
Pathfinder: 1281 & 1282
Landranger: 195

Parking & Starting Point:
Parking is available in the large car parking area amongst the trees at Squirrel's Corner on the B3081 (GR.025152), one mile south east of the crossing of the A354 at Handley traffic island on Bottlebush Down.

Of Interest:
This ride starts in a belt of trees called Lady Shaftesbury's Girdle, that runs for some distance around the estate of Wimborne St Giles. Another section runs through Brockington Beeches and, on the return, runs for a mile along the east side of the Ackling Dyke. Hundreds of trees were uprooted or damaged in the storms of 1987.

At the top of this Drive Plantation the route is crossed by the Dorset Cursus, which was discovered by aerial photographs. This double line of banks is believed to be about 5000 years old and was made by Neolithic tribes as a processional road used when burying their chiefs. All across Wyke and Bottlebush Downs you can see many Long and Round Barrows dating back from 3500 to 2000 BC. Some of these burial mounds were built at high points along the Cursus.

Route Description:

1. From your parking place take the bridleway going south through the trees and over the Downs to the road at Monkton Up Wimborne (GR.019135).

2. Turn right and then left opposite the pillar box to ride up a lane crossing the River Allen. Leave a bridleway on your right and take the first turn left. In 200 yards turn right round a clump of yew trees into a grass lane. *This is a good place for a canter if you wish.* **Follow the bridleway markers left and right around a field edge then right and left through the avenue of Brockington Beeches to a road (GR.016115).**

3. Cross the road with care and keep right and right again up a bridleway, passing a signpost. Turn left down the first green lane which comes out at the Drovers Inn (GR.003106). *This village is Gussage All Saints and the Drovers Inn will make you and your horse most welcome, offering refreshment and a hitching rail.*

4. Ride through the village of Gussage All Saints, past the church and over the stream following the road up the valley until it is crossed by the Ackling Dyke. Turn right up this old Roman road and ride for 0.50 miles (GR.996118).

5. Turn left up the byway, then right past a long barrow to Gussage Hill. At this site of an ancient settlement, turn right to Harley Gap and a junction of 5 bridleways (GR.004135). *There is a memorial stone here to John Ironmonger who was Farm Manager on Lord Shaftesbury's estate for many years. He loved to drive and ride his Welsh Cob here.*

6. Turn left, back on the Ackling Dyke and ride for two miles crossing a road as you do so. *The tree belt runs along the east side of the track until it is crossed by the Neolithic Cursus. From here the Roman embankment, or aggar, is the finest example in this country. On reaching the B3081 on Bottlebush Down you can see the Ackling Dyke continuing for a further mile beside 27 Bronze Age burial mounds; unfortunately the right of way there is a footpath only.*

7. Turn right (GR.016163) and ride along the wide, tree lined, grass verges, to return to your parking place. *There are many reports of phantom horsemen, with bare legs and leather tunics, carrying threatening weapons, galloping around the mounds - keep your eyes peeled for a sighting!*

Trail 17

Bottlebush Down

Monkton Up Wimborne

Harley Gap

Gussage Hill

Yew

Brockington Down

Gussage All Saints

75

A 9 MILE CIRCULAR TRAIL (CLOCKWISE)

Ordnance Survey Maps:
Pathfinder: 1282
Landranger: 184 & 195

Parking & Starting Point:
Parking is available by Pentridge Church (GR.035178). This is found from the A354 Blandford to Salisbury road where you take the Pentridge turning 1.50 miles north of the Handley traffic island. In the village turn right and then right again opposite a notice board where you will see this good parking area.

Of Interest:
The four mile leg from Pentridge Hill into Cranborne and back, is well worth taking as there are some splendid views of Penbury Knoll. If you do not take this option, the ride is reduced to 5 miles in length.

Pentridge means Hill of the Boars and with its church, St Rumbold's, dates back to Celtic times.

Bokerley Ditch and Dyke were defensive earthworks built by the early people of Wessex to keep out the marauding Saxons and still form the Dorset boundary. Beyond this you can have a long gallop across Martin Down where racehorses are trained.

This National Nature Reserve is famous for its butterflies and moths, flowers such as Burnt Tip, Frog and Pyramidal Orchids and birds including larks, nightingales and the rare Montague Harrier.

Cranborne Manor is an elegant Jacobean house enlarged from a medieval hunting lodge by the first Earl of Salisbury. It was the centre of the Cranborne Chase Courts and now has an excellent garden centre. The church was founded in 980AD as a Benedictine Abbey.

Route Description:

1. From your parking place go through a gate on the north side of the parking area and follow the hedge on your left until you meet a road. Turn left, then right on a bend going up a bridleway for 250 yards. Fork left up the lane and ride along three field edges to Woodyates (GR.031193).

2. Turn right up a tarmac farm lane and keep riding straight on through a corn field and gate on to Bokerley Dyke. *If you wish to have a ride around Martin Down, this is where you start.* **Otherwise, follow the bank and ditch round to your right, leaving the first bridleway beside a belt of trees, going back to Pentridge. As the bank rises up a hill, you will take another bridleway running in a dip through it to a junction of four bridleways and the top of Blagdon Hill (GR.054081).**

3. Turn right up a lane and in 50 yards turn left to ride through a small

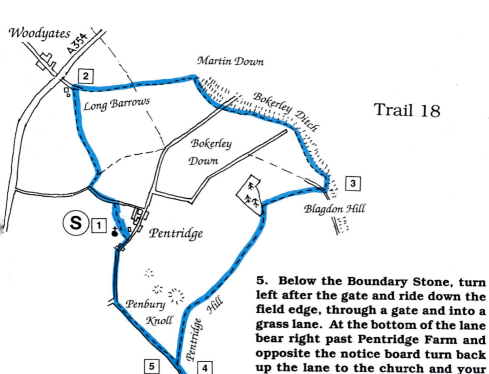

Trail 18

5. Below the Boundary Stone, turn left after the gate and ride down the field edge, through a gate and into a grass lane. At the bottom of the lane bear right past Pentridge Farm and opposite the notice board turn back up the lane to the church and your parking place.

wicket gate and into the trees. **Near the top, with a view over Martin Down, go through a gate and turn left keeping the field fence on the left across Pentridge Hill.** *You will pass the pine trees of Penbury Knoll, Iron Age Hill Fort, on your right from which you can see for miles.* **Go through one gate and on to the next one (GR.038165).**

4. To go to Cranborne go through the gate beside the Boundary Stone and bear left down the bridleway lane for two miles to a short stretch of road to Cranborne Square, where, having taken refreshment if you wish at the Sheaf of Arrows pub in the Market Square, you turn around and return to the Boundary Stone (GR.038165).

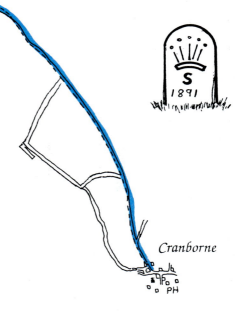

Disclaimer

Whilst all due care was taken in the preparation of these maps neither the British Horse Society nor their agents or servants accept any responsibility for any inaccuracies which may occur. It should be borne in mind that landmarks and conditions change and it is assumed that the user has a Pathfinder or Landranger Ordnance Survey map and a compass.

The Country Code should be observed by every rider, with great care being taken to keep to the line of the Public Rights of Way particularly when crossing farmland.

ISLE OF PURBECK - DORSET

Purbeck, as the locals refer to it, has a unique character all of its own. It is an island by courtesy only. It is really a peninsula at the south east corner of the county. Bounded to the north by the River Frome, Poole Harbour on the east and the English Channel to the south, leaving an imaginary line drawn from Worbarrow Bay to the source of the little stream Luckford Lake, shortly joining the River Frome, all but encircling Purbeck, thus in olden days cutting it off from the rest of Dorset.

In this small area, 12 miles long by 10 miles wide, lies some of the most diverse and rich landscape to be found anywhere in England. To the south, the Dorset Heritage Coast offers some spectacular coastline (parts of which are included in both rides). Between the coast and the Purbeck Hills, lies rich pasture land with ancient stone farmhouses and hamlets, beautiful manor houses, and prominent throughout, the remains of Corfe Castle, destroyed by Oliver Cromwell in the 1640's. To the north of the hills

lies chiefly heathland, gorse and heather and now forestry, and in recent years, Britain's largest onshore oilfield. There are Neolithic Forts and barrows, Roman roads and remains of hunting lodges dating back to King John's time.

The magic of Purbeck for the horseman is its diversity of terrain from steep chalk ridges to grassy slopes sweeping down to the edge of the cliffs, leafy lanes and sandy tracks through heath and forest, the spectacular coastal views, especially from Smedmore Hill and rounding Old Harry Rocks.

The two rides listed can be joined together to make two days riding with an overnight halt. Instructions are included separately should you wish to do this.

NB. It must be noted that this being a coastal area, the high summer, July-August, are not recommended for overnight stays unless they have been booked well in advance!

CHURCH KNOWLE VALLEY RIDE

A 12 MILE CIRCULAR TRAIL (ANTI-CLOCKWISE)

Ordnance Survey Maps:
Outdoor Leisure: 15

Parking & Starting Point:
Parking is available at the Steeple Picnic Area (GR.904817). This is reached from the Wareham By-pass by turning south onto Grange Road. The Park is approximately 4 miles on the left hand side.

NB: There are excellent picnic spots all along the route.

Of Interest:
The Church Knowle Valley Ride offers some of the most varied landscape and spectacular views over the coast line, while passing through isolated Purbeck stone farmsteads, many dating back to the Domesday Book, along leafy lanes and chalk ridges. It is mostly grassy track with some quite steep gradients. There is approximately one mile of tarmac road.

Wild flowers abound in the spring - bluebells, cowslips, primroses, early purple orchids, followed by bee orchids and pyramid orchids in June. Sweet smelling thyme and harebells and honeysuckles fill the air with scent in summer.

Buzzards and kestrels abound and near the cliffs, you might be lucky enough to see a peregrine.

Route Description:

1. Leave the parking area to the east and just outside the park, at the beginning of the Ridgeway Track, turn right down the hill, following the waymarker. This steep path meets the road. Turn left and follow the road for 300 yards and where it bends left take the farm track which is straight ahead and follow the waymarkers.

2. Ride straight down through Steeple Leaze Farm and cross Corfe River over the small sleeper bridge. For a short distance here, the track is rough and stony. Keep on the track through rough ground onto the ridge. Go through the gate and ride across the field at an angle to the right to meet the wire fence close to the Range Boundary gate. Turn left (GR.908803) along the ridge, keeping the wire on the right for 0.75 miles to come out on Kimmeridge/Steeple Lane. *This section offers fantastic views over Kimmeridge Bay and Smedmore House.*

Turn right and then immediately take the first left turn. In 50 yards (GR.919802) turn right up a track to Smedmore Hill and on to Swyre Head (GR.934785). Keep the wall, or hedge, on the right all the way. *There are unrivalled views from all along here; to the north the Church Knowle Valley, Corfe Castle and beyond; to the south and west, Kimmeridge Bay and the magnificent Gad Cliff, and on down past*

Trail 19

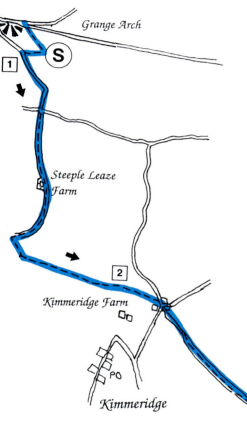

Grange Arch

S

1

Steeple Leaze Farm

2

Kimmeridge Farm

PO

Kimmeridge

3. From Swyre Head turn north keeping the wall on the left, skirting the Golden Bowl that encloses Encombe House. *There are fine views here of the House and St. Aldhelms Head.*

At the next gate (GR.942789) at the end of Polar Wood, keep down across the centre of the field, on the track to the gate (GR.944793). *There is a good view of Poole Harbour from here.*

4. After coming through the gate, do not turn right on the drive, but keep straight ahead and turn right at the T-junction on the lane. Follow the lane to the edge of Kingston village. *The very fine church is on the right and well worth a visit.* **Just before the first cottage on the left hand side, turn left, riding back on yourself and take a track down through the woods.**

There is an excellent public house in Kingston, The Scott Arms. Both horses and riders are welcomed, but it is best avoided in high summer when it can be very busy.

Lulworth Cove - White Nothe, Chesil Bank, Portland and Weymouth. Possibly the most spectacular and unspoilt section of the south coast. Swyre Head offers a pleasant halt for a breather. Hearsay has it that the little knoll marking the highest point was erected due to rivalry between two great Purbeck families to have the highest point in Purbeck on their estate.

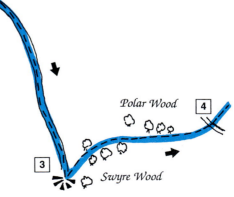

Smedmore Hill

Polar Wood

4

3

Swyre Wood

5. Go through the gate on the edge of the wood and bear right riding down hill on the very stony track and through fields to Blashenwell Farm. *There are beautiful views of Corfe Castle and Poole Harbour and beyond from this point.*

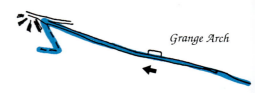

Grange Arch

6. Follow the track right through the farmyard and out, leaving the house and duck pond on the right.

7. Keep along the track and ride for about 0.50 miles following it round to the right and through the gate next to the cattle grid onto Corfe Common. Follow the road across Corfe Common.

8. At the next cattle grid, do not go through the gate but turn left (GR.958844) and ride alongside the hedge for about 400 yards and go down the steep slope to Corfe River. Take the ancient little pack horse bridge (GR.956815) over the river, go straight across the next field, through a gate and slightly right across the next field. In 150 yards go through the gate and onto the Church Knowle to Corfe Castle road.

9. Turn left on to the road. In 100 yards turn right through a gate onto the waymarked bridleway.

10. Follow the track passing through one field with the hedge on the right. Then go through a metal gate on to the base of the hill. Turn right (GR.946823) eastwards along the bottom of the hill. In 150 yards go through the next gate. In 20 yards turn left and ride back up the hill and through another gate and thence onto Knowle Hill. *You will now actually be back in the same enclosure, but heading westwards.*

11. *Enjoy the fine views back to Corfe Castle and over the Church Knowle Valley to Kingston, Swyre Head and Smedmore where you have ridden from.* **Ride westward, follow the track across the field, through the next gate and keep straight on through a bridle gate. Keep riding straight on again to a bridle gate and onto the lane (GR.932822) for about 30 yards.**

12. Keep riding straight on through the gate and along the ridge. In about 0.50 miles the track bears right. Go left through the bridlegate (GR.924818). *On a clear day there is a good view of the Needles on the Isle of Wight.* **Turn right again and ride along the ridge, Ridgeway Hill, with the fence now on the right. Go through the next bridlegate and straight on again. In about 0.25 miles look for Grange Arch on the right.** *This is a folly built in the 1750's by the Bond family. It is believed never to have been finished, but it does offer fine views over the Grange and heathland to the north. It is here that legend tells that in 1678 a great army was seen marching along the ridgeway and warnings were sent to Wareham and then London, that England had been invaded. It was reputed to have been seen at other times of pending national disaster.*

Ride along for 0.50 miles to return to your parking place.

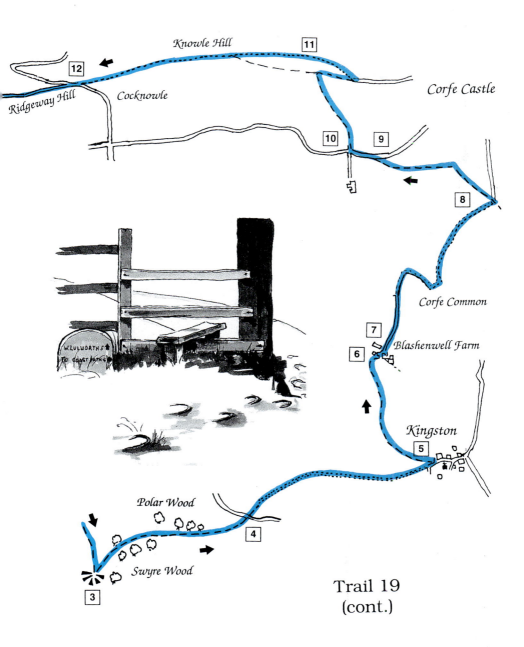

Knowle Hill

| 11 |

| 12 |

Ridgeway Hill

Cocknowle

Corfe Castle

| 10 |

| 9 |

| 8 |

Corfe Common

| 7 |

Blashenwell Farm

| 6 |

Kingston

| 5 |

Polar Wood

| 4 |

Swyre Wood

| 3 |

Trail 19
(cont.)

W. LULWORTH 5
TO COAST PATH

corfe castle

OLD HARRY ROCKS

**A 17.5 MILE CIRCULAR TRAIL
(ANTI-CLOCKWISE)**

Ordnance Survey Maps:
Outdoor Leisure: 15

Parking & Starting Points:
Parking is available in two lay-bys on
the edge of a forestry lane just before
the start (GR.974842). This is reached
by taking the Wareham By-pass
towards Swanage A350. Just before
Corfe Castle, turn left for Studland. In
0.50 miles take the first left turn signed
Wytch and follow along the narrow lane
for 0.75 miles to the lay-bys. Take care
not to block forestry entrances.

Of Interest:
*The Old Harry rocks ride takes you
through very varied terrain, forestry and
heathland, chalk downland with
fantastic views over Poole Harbour and
Purbeck. The highlight being the section
down to and around Old Harry Rocks
where the scenery is superb. It is mostly
grass and sandy tracks with
approximately 1.50 miles of tarmac.*

Route Description:

**1. Leave the parking area and
retrace your tracks up the lane to the
Studland road. Turn left, cross the
road and turn immediately right.
Follow the track up past Rollington
Farm, keeping straight onto the hill.
The track curves left handed onto
the top of the ridge (GR.973822).**

This is the point at which the ride
would join Route 19 - Church Knowle
Valley Ride.

**Turn left and go through the gate to
the right of the Radio Relay mast
onto Rollington Hill.** *There is a fine
view looking back westwards over the
historic village of Corfe Castle, with the
castle in the foreground to the right,
majestically guarding the entrance to
Purbeck.*

**2. Continue riding straight on
through the next field to the
bridlegate. Keep the fence on the
left all the way to the next gate. Go
straight ahead on to Brenscombe
Hill. Remain on the ridge keeping
straight on. Pass tumuli and a long
barrow on the left, Ailwood Down,
(GR.001814). Going through two
more gates will bring you to the trig
point (GR.000813), Nine Barrow
Down. The track bears right going
down the hill skirting Godlingston
Hill and into the valley and comes
out onto the Swanage to Studland
road.**

**3. Turn left onto the road
(GR.018812). Ride WITH CARE for
150 yards along the road, which can
be busy. Just after the junction
there is a wide grass verge which
goes all the way to the entrance to
the bridleway on the right hand side.
Look for the National Trust signs.
Cross the road (GR.020816).**

4. Take the track which goes

straight up the hill, bear left at the top towards the obelisk. Go through the bridlegate next to the obelisk and proceed eastwards along the ridge. *Beware of the remains of iron posts which are in the track about 100 yards from the gate.* Continue in a straight line on through the next gate with the fence on the left. Keep straight on again, ignoring the bridleway that crosses over from north to south and go through the gate to continue until you come to the next gate close to the Trig Point (GR.045813). Take the small bridlegate nearest to the Trig Point, the fence will now be on the right.

From here there is an excellent view right the way up the Solent past the Isle of Wight, across Poole Harbour and Swanage Bay. In the foreground will be Old Harry Rocks, once connected to the Isle of Wight at the Needles, and Studland Bay.

5. Follow the fence until you reach the next bridlegate, just to the left is a water trough. Go through this and you will be on open downland sweeping down to Old Harry Rocks. *Please keep to the path as this area is undergoing a programme of restoration back to old downland turf by the National Trust. From here to Studland village you may encounter many walkers - please be courteous to them.*

6. Follow the track down to Old Harry Rocks. The track follows the cliff to the left and goes through a little wood along the edge of a small field; it gets quite narrow here. Look for the waymarked footpath to the right where you carry straight on until you reach the small bridlegate just ahead of you. Go through the gate and follow the track for 100 yards to the lane.

Just before you come out on to the lane there is a block of public conveniences (GR.038825) and there is room to tie up horses! You will also find the Bankes Arms Country Inn 200 yards on, to the right, where you can obtain refreshments.

7. Coming out into the lane, turn left and follow it round the War Memorial, bearing left into School Lane and riding the 100 yards to the Swanage to Studland road. Cross straight over and in 150 yards take the track to the right, waymarked to Greenland (GR.033825).

8. Follow the track on the edge of the heath and fields until it meets a stony track. Turn left and go through the Wadmoor Farm complex. Continue on the track through a ford and follow the bridleway signs onto open heathland. *On the left you can see the Agglestone Rock, dropped by the devil in a fit of rage, or so the story goes, as the make up of the rock is not from this area at all.* Keep straight on this track, ignoring the track to the right, and riding straight ahead until a bridlegate is reached which is almost in a stream. Go through the gate and follow the track for about 300 yards through some furze until fields are reached and another bridlegate.

9. Go through this gate and bear half right across the field to a second bridlegate. Keeping the same line, ride to the corner of the field and a third bridlegate. Go through this and keep straight on. Ignore the bridleway sign to Rempstone. Ride straight on going through three more

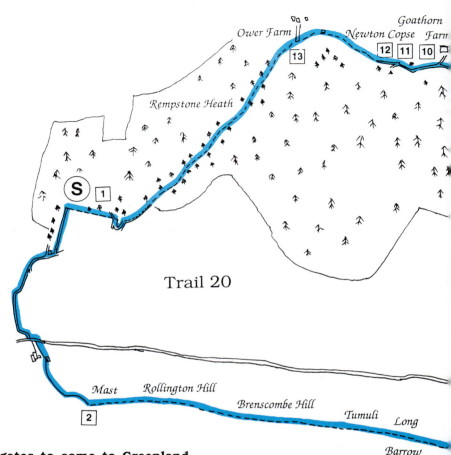

Trail 20

bridlegates to come to Greenland. Just after the two barns on the right, you will meet a stony track. Turn left here and follow the track looking for bridleway signs. In 0.50 miles bear left, where the track goes half right to Goat Horn Farm (GR.013848).

10. In a short distance you will join a bigger hard track which comes in from the right. *This is still a bridleway used by BP for their oil traffic, so take care.* In 200 yards there is a good verge on the left hand side. At the next corner, the main track bears away to the left but you ride straight ahead (GR.008848).

11. Ride straight on until the track opens out. There is a fence and a locked gate on the right. Straight ahead is the entrance to Newton Cottage. This is the bridleway. Ride along as if going to the house, through the garden, down the drive leaving the house on the right and so through the bridlegate into the fields beyond. *Newton Bay is on the right. This is a very pretty and quiet place for a picnic.*

12. Follow the track across the fields, through one gate and into

88

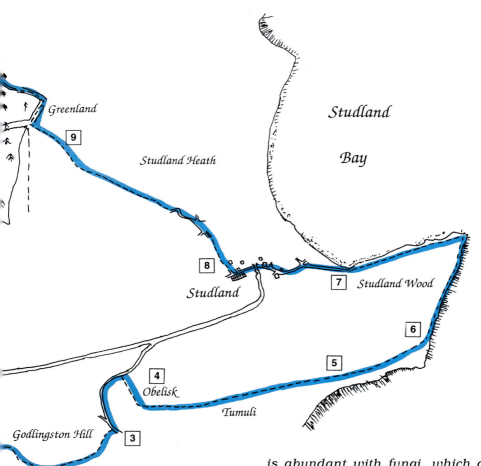

Greenland

9

Studland Heath

Studland Bay

8

Studland

7 Studland Wood

6

5

4

Obelisk

Tumuli

Godlingston Hill

3

---

another field to a second gate leading out onto a stony track. Ower Farm is to the right.

These old tracks are reputed to have been used by smugglers, with pack ponies, carrying contraband to Ower Quay, or even Wareham, in order to avoid the main roads and the Revenue Men!

13. Once on the stony track, keep riding straight on crossing a small river and entering the forestry. *This* is abundant with fungi, which are especially interesting in the autumn. **Ride straight across a tarmac lane following the bridleway signs. Stay on this main track, which is mainly gravel but becomes sandy. Do not deviate to right or left. At the junction (GR.984842), bear right. The track comes out onto a tarmac lane, past a house on the left and a farm on the right. 50 yards after the farm there is a T-junction, turn right following the bridleway signs along the tarmac track.**

Ride on for about 0.25 miles and turn right to return to your starting point.

INSTRUCTIONS FOR LINKING ROUTES 19 & 20

If you wish to link route 19, Church Valley Ride with route 20, The Old Harry Rocks Ride, proceed as below:

8. At the next cattle grid, do not go through the gate, but turn right and ride across the open common. Follow the grass track keeping slightly right with the hedge away on your left, riding on open ground. Ahead of you is a gate leading onto the Corfe Castle to Kingston road. Go through this gate and on to the road and turn left. In 20 yards, at the T-junction, cross the Corfe Castle to Swanage road and turn right. Ride for 10 yards and turn left through a gate onto a small common.

9. Ride straight ahead following the track up over a bridge crossing the railway line and into a field. Go half right, keeping the fence on the right, and ride up across the field. When the hedge comes down to meet the fence on the right, go left up along the hedge. At the junction of this hedge with the one coming across in front, turn right through the gap and ride up to a small gate on the top of the rise.

10. Go through this gate and turn left to ride across the field to meet Woolgarston Lane (GR.976813). Turn left and ride up the lane past some houses. At the T-junction turn left into Underhill Lane. In 300 yards turn right onto a track signposted Rollington Hill.

11. Go up the track and through the gate, bear left up the hill join The Old Harry Rocks Ride (GR.973822) and continue your ride at Section 1 of route 20.

If you are riding from route 20, The Old Harry Rocks Ride into route 19, The Church Knowle Valley Ride proceed as follows from Rollington Hill (GR.973822).

1. Go through the second gate to the right of the Radio Relay mast. Ride down the hill and follow the track through the gate down to the Underhill Lane. Turn left. In 300 yards turn right down the hill along Woolgarston Lane passing houses. Just after the only house on the right take the metal gate ahead on the right (GR.976813). Ride up the field to the hedge keeping the hedge to the right. In 30 yards turn right and go through the bridlegate.

2. Ride down the edge of the field keeping the hedge on the right. Go through the gap where the hedges meet and turn left to go down the field. Where the fence comes in front, bear right and keep the fence on the left to come to a bridge over the railway.

3. Ride over the bridge and follow the track down to a gate leading onto the Swanage to Corfe Castle road. Cross the road, and turn left up the Corfe Castle to Kingston road. In 20 yards, turn right across the road through a gate leading onto Corfe Common. Ride straight ahead, then go slightly right across open ground. The hedge will be on the right and getting closer all the time until you reach a gate with a cattle grid at No. 8 of the Church Knowle Valley Ride. Here ride straight ahead with the hedge on the right and in 200 yards go down the steep slope to Corfe River from where you continue to follow the Church Knowle Valley ride directions.

The
Bankes Arms
Hotel

Studland, Dorset

Telephone: 01929 450225

As horse lovers who breed and race our own stock, we offer a warm welcome to this lovely part of the Dorset coast. We have wonderful riding through the forestry and heathland all year and from Oct-March, beach riding along 4.5 miles of golden sands is available.

The accommodation is en-suite with sea views, colour T.V., tea making etc. Log fires, real ales, good extensive menu, and grazing for your own horses. Stabling, and also horses for hire can be arranged through the local riding establishment. For a brochure, please ring **01929 450225** and ask for details quoting "Dorset on Horseback."

GOLD HILL ORGANIC FARM

Childe Okeford, Blandford Forum, Dorset, DT11 8HB.

Enjoy a whole week with your horses - no extra charge.
A choice of 23 rides, or explore at your leisure.
Ample free parking for horsebox.
Clean pasture, or stable.
Able to graze with sheep or cattle an advantage.
Charming, well equipped, light and airy ground floor annex
for 2 non-smokers.
For brochures contact: D.N & A.D. Cross.
Telephone No: 01258 860 293

A 13 MILE CIRCULAR TRAIL (ANTI-CLOCKWISE)

Ordnance Survey Maps:
Outdoor Leisure: 15

Parking & Starting Points:
Parking is available by prior arrangement with Gerry or Nina Evans at the Countryman Inn, East Knighton (GR.810857), which is just off the A352. Turn up Blacknoll Lane, next to the Rainbow Garage. Please telephone (01305) 852666.

Of Interest:
The Dorset Heritage Coast is famous for its beautiful coastline and fine views over the rolling chalk downs. It is patterned with small hedge lined fields and Thomas Hardy's Edgon Heath of heather and gorse and the River Frome Valley and many more well known beauty spots such as Lulworth Cove and of course the Castle, along with Durdle Door and the sheltered bays of Weymouth and Portland. There are many hill forts and burial barrows from Neolithic times. Some roads still follow the pattern laid down by the Romans. The White Horse at Osmington was cut into the chalk in 1815 and represents George III on his charger. This was cut in celebration of his visit to Weymouth.

Route Description:

1. From your parking place at the Countryman Inn, ride towards the A352 to turn left just before the road along a track signposted to Knighton

Farm. Ride for approximately 200 yards along the track and turn right at the crossroads of bridleways to cross the A352 into East Knighton Lane. Ride along this lane until you reach the T-junction in Winfrith Newburgh. Turn left into the High Street. At the end of the village bear right on the corner by the Church, signed to Chaldon Herring and then take the first track on the right onto

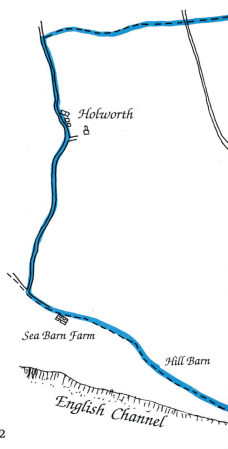

Holworth

Sea Barn Farm

Hill Barn

English Channel

the bridleway leading to **Wynards.** **Take the left hand fork to Five Marys.** *Five Marys is a Neolithic Barrow and from here you can see the village of Chaldon Herring in the valley below. Refreshments can be obtained at the Sailors Return in Chaldon Herring, when you should note the amusing public house sign.*

2. **On reaching the third metalled road, turn left onto the road and ride for about one mile to reach the coastal bridleway (GR.763820). Turn left.** *There are beautiful views of* Weymouth Bay, Portland and Ringstead Bay from here. You can also see the beach that appears in Thomas Hardy's short story "The Distracted Preacher".

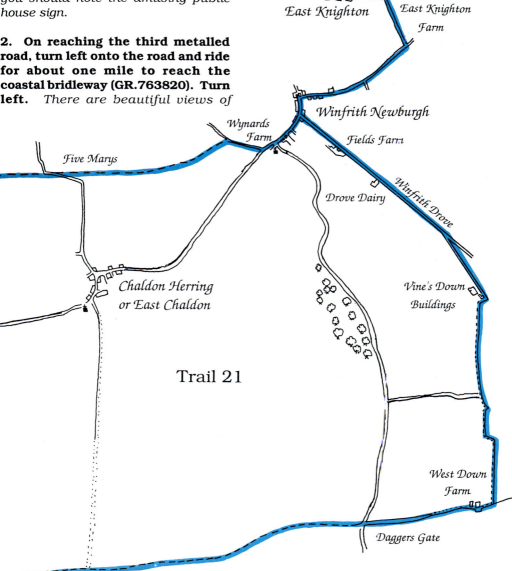

Follow this bridleway eastwards for about three miles to Winfrith Newburgh and West Lulworth. On reaching the road at Daggers Gate (GR.811814), go straight over to the track and after 0.50 miles pass West Down Farm. Turn left and follow the permissive bridleway into Winfrith High Street. Turn right and then right again at the village shop into School Lane which eventually becomes East Knighton Lane and so retrace your steps to the Countryman Inn.

THE DORSET DOWNS

These high chalk hills run south west from Cranborne Chase across the centre of Dorset. They separate the heathland of Thomas Hardy country, running from Verwood to Dorchester, from the lush meadowland of the Blackmore Vale to the north and Marshwood Vale to the west.

As the ancient springy turf on the slopes is too steep for cultivation centuries of sheep grazing have encouraged many wild flowers such as the bee orchid and cowslip, and insects such as the Adonis Blue butterfly.

There are many splendid viewpoints from the downs and on some hilltops the chalk grasslands give way to flinty clay.

Many of the houses and walls in this area are built with alternate layers of flintstone and brick, and lots of cottages are thatched.

This is splendid riding country with miles of open grass tracks alternating with deep wooded combes where the deer live.

A 7 MILE HILLY, CIRCULAR TRAIL (CLOCKWISE)

Ordnance Survey Maps:
Pathfinder: 1281 & 1300
Landranger: 194

Parking & Starting Points:
Parking is available in a wide tarmac lay-by, set behind a grass verge with plenty of room to park and unload horses. The lay-by is two miles north west of Blandford, just above Durweston, on the west side of the A357 (GR.855090).

Of Interest:
The River Stour cuts right through the chalk hills between these villages. Both Hod and Hambledon Hills are Iron Age Hill Forts crowned with huge earthworks, with marvellous views from the top. In 44AD Vespasian led the Romans to defeat the native tribes and he built a camp for 600 Roman soldiers on the north east corner of Hod Hill.

A minor road runs between this and Hambledon Hill, where in 1645, 2000 Dorset locals gathered in protest against both Royalists and Parliamentarians and petitioned them to stop the Civil War. They were eventually routed by 50 of Cromwell's Dragoons.

Route Description:

1. From your parking place ride towards Durweston and take the first lane on the left opposite Wynchard Bank and then bear left round the mill. **Pass the mill pond and turn right through a gate and cross a field to the bridge going over the River Stour.** *You may need to dismount to open the gates.* **Follow the lane under the railway bridge, leaving a footpath on the left, bear right to a metal gate opening on to the A350.** *Care here, the traffic can be fast as you turn left* **(GR.862093).**

2. Just past the White Horse public house, turn left and ride through Stourpaine and turn down the second lane on the right opposite a playing field. Hod Drive runs for 1.25 miles between fields and then goes into Hod Wood, above the river. Where the path divides; the upper track is dryer and both tracks will bring you on to a minor road (GR.853113).

3. Turn right and ride for 200 yards. Just past Keepers Cottage, turn left through a gate and climb up the field edge to a barn. Turn left through a gate and follow the bridleway along the ridge of the hill for 0.50 miles until you meet the Ridgeway, waymarked by the Wessex Wyvern. Turn right through a hunting gate and follow the fenced path to the trig. point. *This is the site of a Neolithic Camp.* **Turn right (GR.848123).**

4. Ride down the track and through a new gate to come to a wall. Leave the Ridgeway here and turn right (GR.858124).

5. **Follow the line of the wall until reaching a gate and then keep straight on with the hedge on your left, not uphill, and go through two wooden gates and fields to come to a road (GR.859112).** *Watch out for deep earth holes here.*

6. **Turn right and ride up the road past Keeper's Cottage. Go through the gate on the left and keep right on the bridleway up the hill to the gate beside the trees.** *There is an information board here at the entrance to Hod Hill Fort.* **Ride across the top. Enjoy the splendid views in all directions and then go through a gate into a lane (GR.861099).**

7. *Here your horse can enjoy a drink and a paddle before making your way down to Stourpaine.* **Turn left at the Old School House and retrace your route back past the White Horse public house to your parking place at Durweston.** *The White Horse Inn offers excellent refreshment and welcomes riders - you should find a hitching rail there for your horse.*

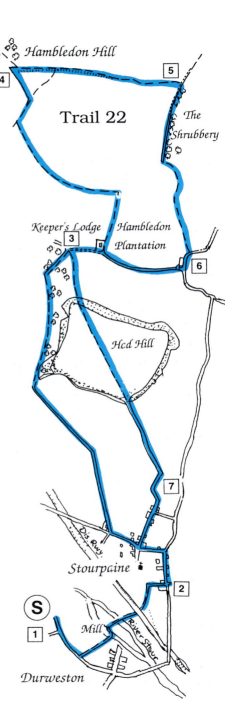

RIDE WITH:

CARE

- For the Land

COURTESY

- To other users

CONSIDERATION

- For the Farmer

AN 8 MILE CIRCULAR TRAIL (ANTI-CLOCKWISE)

Ordnance Survey Maps:
Pathfinder: 1300
Landranger: 194

Parking & Starting Points:
Parking is available in a wide tarmac lay-by, set behind a grass verge, with plenty of room to park and unload horses. The lay-by is two miles northwest of Blandford, just above Durweston, on the west side of the A357 (GR.855090).

Of Interest:
There is great local rivalry between the villagers of Durweston and Stourpaine at their annual cricket match. They also hold a famous tug-of-war across the River Stour, where the losers get a ducking in the river.

This ride climbs up through a lovely wooded combe past Shepherd's Corner Farm where, as the name suggests, sheep farming is the main occupation on the higher slopes. The return route follows the drift of bluebells in the Hanging Woods above Bryanstone School. This grand mansion was built in the 1890's for Viscount Portman, founder of the pack of foxhounds still known today as the Portman Hunt.

Route Description:

1. From your parking place ride down into Durweston and turn right round the War Memorial. After the left bend, turn right and ride up a field track by Sutcombe Knap. Continue riding up through the woods joining a road past the converted Folly Barn and follow this road as far as Shepherd's Corner Farm (GR.835079).

2. Continue riding straight on up a green lane for 2.25 miles, going through a gate until you come to a road (GR.826069). Turn left.

3. At the first bend, turn right (GR.826069) up a farm lane and ride past some barns. Turn down the first lane on the left (GR.817068) and climb up to a T-junction. Turn right, then left below a group of trees, to join a road (GR.825073).

Turnworth

3

Hedge End

Pond Down Buildings

4

4. Turn left to Hedge End Farm and cross straight over this road and up a track beside Field Grove Wood. Ride on until you meet a lane (GR.841064).

5. Cross over into Blackfern Plantation riding past a Forest Enterprise fir cone sign. Keep right on the field edge track for 0.50 miles until meeting a road where you turn left to the signpost (GR.851064).

6. Take the left Durweston road. *Enjoy the splendid views to the hills round Blandford along this track.* **Turn right on the far side of a belt of trees and follow this bridleway down for one mile, going through a gate between fields. (GR.864076).**

7. Turn left through a gate above Four Acre Coppice. *Here there is a chance to canter on the lovely grass.* When the trees end, turn right and go through the first metal gate on the right and ride down the side of the school playing fields (GR.859085).

8. Turn left and ride through the village, turning right and left in the centre, past the War Memorial to return to your starting point.

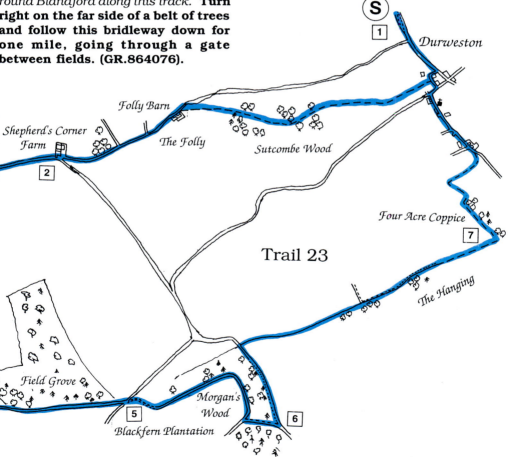

Trail 23

AN 11 MILE CIRCULAR TRAIL (CLOCKWISE)

Ordnance Survey Maps:
Pathfinder: 1299 & 1300
Landranger: 194

Parking & Starting Points:
Parking is available in a car park on Bulbarrow Hill (GR.784058). This is by a crossroads where a stone marks the second highest point in Dorset at 902 feet. There is another wide grass parking area just to the west, in front of the masts.

Of Interest:
For the first mile of your ride, there are splendid views from the ridge above Woolland and Ibberton over lush pastures of Blackmoor Vale.

Bridleways then cross just below Winterborne Houghton through a trout farm. This is the highest of a dozen villages which take their name from this stream, which often runs dry in summer.

From Milton Park Wood the route runs down to the magnificent Milton Abbey which was established by King Athelstan in 932 AD as a college of canons but six years later became a Benedictine Monastery. After a lightning strike in 1309 it was rebuilt and extended until in 1539 the abbey buildings were granted to Sir John Tregonwell by Henry VIII. In 1771 Lord Milton had a large gothic house built overlooking some 100 houses, 3 pubs and a school at Middleton. These displeased him so

when Capability Brown had laid out the gardens he was asked to design the twenty double cob and thatched cottages of Milton Abbas, out of sight on the hill, and the old town was demolished to make way for a large lake.

Route Description:

1. Set off along the road to Ibberton Hill where there is a wide grass picnic area. Opposite a bridleway sign on the left, turn right up a farm track and go through a field gate. Follow the bridleway signs first right then left around South Down to Coombe Bottom (GR.817068).

2. Just before some barns, turn right and climb up to a T-junction. Turn right on a gravel track, then left, below a group of trees, to meet a road (GR.817056).

3. Cross this road and ride through two narrow gates and fields down to a fish farm. *Here you can see numerous trout in open ponds below Winterborne Houghton.* **Cross over and go up a steep hill. Watch out for rabbit burrows in a bank on your right. Ride on until you meet a third road (GR.824039).**

4. Keep straight on for 400 yards into Charity Wood. Turn left at the T-junction and then right at the next crossroads between an avenue of ancient beech trees. Cross a track in a dip and ride on until you see a bridleway arrow turning off left down

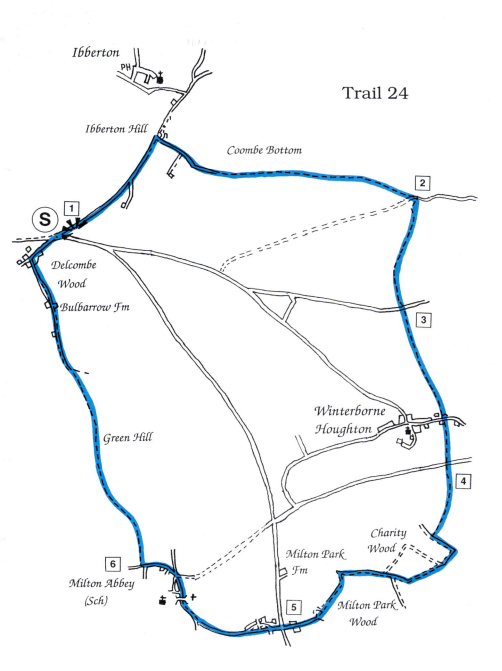

Trail 24

Ibberton

PH

Ibberton Hill

Coombe Bottom

2

S 1

Delcombe Wood

Bulbarrow Fm

3

Green Hill

Winterborne Houghton

4

Charity Wood

Milton Park Fm

6

Milton Abbey (Sch)

5

Milton Park Wood

a narrow path which you follow. Go straight over another main path and wind left, then right, on the edge of the wood, looking across to Park Farm Museum. Turn right on a main forest track and follow this round and on up to a crossroads (GR.811022).

5. *If you wish to take refreshments then a 0.25 mile detour by turning left then right, can be made into Milton Abbas and the Hambro Arms.*

To continue the ride cross carefully into Catherine's Well. *This is a wide road of modern houses which could be used to park a horsebox.* **Continue downhill and then straight ahead on a tarmac road, past Milton Abbey School and playing fields (GR.795026).**

6. Take the bridleway on the right going up through woods and Green Hill Down Nature Reserve. Keep riding straight on through fields of sheep, past Bulbarrow Farm and timber yard. Turn right on a road round Delcombe Wood to return to your start.

ETHERIDGE FARM

Ideally situated in a bridleway
network of fabulous rides.

★ ★ ★

Excellent accommodation
is available for Horse and Rider.

★ ★ ★

You will be assured of
a most enjoyable visit.

★ ★ ★

Darknoll Lane, Okeford Fitzpaine,
Blandford Forum, Dorset, DT11 0RP
Telephone: 01258 860037

POUND COTTAGE RIDING CENTRE

Luccombe Farm, Milton Abbas,
Blandford, Dorset, DT11 0BD.
Tel: 01258 880057

Stabling available

◆ ◆ ◆

Escorted hacking on our horses

◆ ◆ ◆

Local B&B can be arranged

◆ ◆ ◆

BHS & ABRS
approved establishment

INSURANCE:

The BHS recommends that before undertaking any of these routes, both horse and rider be adequately insured against **THIRD PARTY PUBLIC LIABILITY.** Membership of the BHS gives automatic Third Party Insurance with an indemnity of up to £2,000,000.

BULBARROW HILL, DORSETSHIRE GAP & ANSTY CROSS

TRAIL 25

A 9 MILE CIRCULAR RIDE (ANTI-CLOCKWISE)

Ordnance Survey Maps:
Pathfinder: 1299
Landranger: 194

Parking & Starting Points:
Parking is available at Bulbarrow Hill, on an area of grass at the corner of the triangle of roads just to the west of the radio masts (GR.776057)

Of Interest:
The first three miles of this ride follows the Wessex Ridgeway and is waymarked with blue arrows and the Wessex Wyvern sign of a two legged dragon which has historic links with this area. It is depicted as the sign of King Harold on the Bayeux Tapestry.

The ride starts by going across the Iron Age Rawlesbury Camp, the second highest hill fort in Dorset where a post is all that remains of a cross erected some 30 years ago. After crossing a stream bottom, the route runs up Norden Hill and westwards as far as the Dorsetshire Gap. Although far from any modern road, this break in the chalk hills is the crossing place of many ancient tracks, with ditches, dykes and burial grounds. It probably dates back to pre-Roman times. Beside the signpost is a tin box holding a book which has been signed by visitors from all over the world.

As the route turns back eastwards you will come to Ansty Cross. From here you may divert for 0.25 miles to the famous

Fox Inn for refreshment. Opposite the Fox Inn there used to be an old malt house and brewery which was serviced by teams of shire horses and wagons. The final section of the ride runs north up the lovely valley above Hilton village.

Route Directions:

1. From your parking place take the Stoke Wake road and follow this until you come to a gate on the left with a Ridgeway sign on it. Go through the gate and ride across Rawlesbury Camp to the left of the post. After admiring the view, go through a hunting gate and ride straight ahead across three fields and a stream, to meet a road at Crockers Farm (GR.756050).

2. Cross over the road and ride up a farm lane to ride diagonally across three fields which are separated by gates, then at the bottom hedge, turn left and ride around this field and into Breach Wood. Take the track through trees and carry straight on up a tarmac road then through the yard of Melcombe Park Farm (GR.751033).

3. At the Ridgeway sign above Cony-gar Copse, turn right and follow the track to Dorset Gap. Continue going through a hunting gate and over a headland to go down into the hollow. Savour the atmosphere and sign the visitors' book before retracing your steps to Cony-gar Copse. Keeping above the farm, cross a field going

diagonally to the left and through the gate to join Cothayes Lane which is to the left of the farmhouse. Ride down the lane for 0.25 miles (GR.761034).

4. Turn left and go through a metal hunting gate and cross a stream, following a bridleway. Ride straight on going through three more gates until you join the road at the top at **Ansty Cross.** *If you require refreshments then turn right here and ride down to the Fox Inn.* **The route follows three roads signed to Milton Abbas, as far as a bridleway crossing at the top of the hill (GR.776036).**

5. Turn left into a field and keeping alongside the hedge on your left, go through a gate into the next field, loop back to the right through a second gate in the same hedge further to the east and ride

diagonally to the right and go through a gate by a ruined barn. Follow this grass path on down through two more gates and then turn right to go past Manor Farm and cross over the stream. (GR.781035).

6. Take the bridleway to the left along Hilton Bottom. At the second barn, bear right through a gate and then climb to the left above Hilton Wood to join Ice Drove to the road at the top (GR.778054).

7. Carry on going left and then right up Cuckoo Lane, past the radio masts, to the start and your parking place.

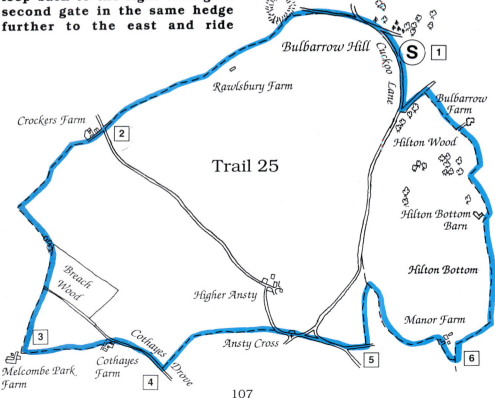

107

THE BRITISH HORSE SOCIETY

The British Horse Society was founded in 1947 when two separate equestrian bodies - The National Horse Association and the Institute of the Horse and Pony Club - decided to join forces and work together for the good of both horse and rider.

It is a marriage that has proved to be a great success and the British Horse Society has steadily increased its membership from just 4000 in the late 1960's to over 60,000 in the 1990's.

By becoming members of the British Horse Society, horse lovers know they are joining a body of people with a shared interest in the horse. Members can be sure that they are contributing to the work of an equine charity with a primary aim to improve the standards of care for horses and ponies. Welfare is not only about the rescuing of horses in distress (which we do); it is also about acting to prevent abuse in the first place. There are many means to achieving this: by teaching and advising, by looking to the horse's well-being and safety, by providing off-road riding, by encouraging high standards in all equestrian establishments, and fighting for the horse's case with government and in Europe.

The British Horse Society works tirelessly towards these aims thanks to the work of its officials at Stoneleigh and its army of dedicated volunteers out in the field.

Membership benefits the horse lover as well as the horse; the Society can offer something to all equestrians, whether they are weekend riders, interested spectators or keen competitors. The benefits include free Third Party Public Liability and Personal Accident insurance, free legal advice, free publications, reductions to British Horse Society events, special facilities at the major shows, and free advice and information on any equine query.

Largely financed by its membership subscriptions, the Society welcomes the support of all horse lovers. If you are thinking of joining the Society and would like to find out more about our work, please contact the Membership Department at the following address:

The British Horse Society
British Equestrian Centre
Stoneleigh Park
Kenilworth
Warwickshire
CV8 2LR
(Telephone: 01203 696697)
Registered Charity No. 210504